The Renters' Rights Act

The Renters' Rights Act: A Practical Guide provides a comprehensive analysis of the most significant reform to residential tenancy law in England in over 30 years. This timely resource explains the abolition of Section 21 no-fault evictions, the conversion of fixed-term tenancies to periodic arrangements and the new regulatory framework designed to rebalance power between landlords and tenants during a housing crisis.

This book covers the historical context of residential tenancy law, details the new grounds for possession, explains strengthened tenant rights regarding rent increases and property conditions and outlines the new Private Rented Sector Ombudsman service. Additional chapters address discrimination protections, the Decent Homes Standard, implications for mortgagees and ground landlords, enforcement mechanisms and anticipated changes to court procedures as the legislation is implemented.

This practical guide is written for a professional audience including residential landlords, property management agents, real estate and litigation lawyers, housing authorities and surveyors operating in England. While primarily serving those who need to understand and implement the new legislation professionally, this book's clear structure and plain language approach make it accessible to academics studying housing policy and legal professionals advising clients on residential property matters.

V. Charles Ward is a UK-registered solicitor and Legal Associate of the Royal Town Planning Institute, currently working on contract with HB Public Law (a local authority shared legal service). He is also Company Solicitor with The Institute of Cemetery and Crematorium Management. His primary professional expertise is in real estate, town and country planning, housing regeneration, company law, and burial and cremation. The author's professional background is primarily (but not exclusively) in the public sector. He has also worked for Capsticks Solicitors as well as Unilever. Earlier books written by this author include *Housing Regeneration: A Plan for Implementation*, *Fire Safety Law* and *Residential Leaseholders Handbook*.

The Renters' Rights Act

A Practical Guide

V. Charles Ward

Routledge
Taylor & Francis Group
LONDON AND NEW YORK

First published 2026
by Routledge
4 Park Square, Milton Park, Abingdon, Oxon OX14 4RN

and by Routledge
605 Third Avenue, New York, NY 10158

Routledge is an imprint of the Taylor & Francis Group, an informa business

British Library Cataloguing-in-Publication Data
A catalogue record for this book is available from the British Library

ISBN: 9781041148951 (hbk)
ISBN: 9781041158288 (pbk)
ISBN: 9781003681403 (ebk)

DOI: 10.1201/9781003681403

Typeset in Times New Roman
by codeMantra

Contents

Preface

The Renters' Rights Act 2025 represents the biggest shift in residential tenant law since the Housing Act 1988 opened up the residential lettings market on 15 January 1989. In the intervening years, the assured shorthold tenancy became the mainstay of the residential lettings market, with landlords able to unilaterally end a residential letting on as little as two months written notice and without the need to give any reason.

With the abolition of assured shorthold tenancies on 1 May 2026, over four million former assured shorthold tenants overnight became assured periodic tenants with potentially lifetime security of tenure. While this does not mean the end of no-fault eviction, it means that, going forward, any landlord wishing to evict their tenant will not only have to prove one of the new statutory grounds of possession but also have to ensure that their tenancy is documented in a way which allows them to do this.

Contrast the simultaneous outlawing of fixed-term residential lettings, which means that any residential tenant can quit their tenancy at any time on giving as little as two months prior written notice to their landlord. In effect, it is a reversal of the situation that existed before 1 May 2026. Just to complicate matters a little further, the Act is being implemented in stages. The reforms, which took effect on 1 May 2026, will only apply to private residential landlords and will not be extended to registered social landlords until later this year.

The new rules also extend to the way a new prospective letting is marketed. Going forward, it is illegal to market a residential letting without quoting a fixed rent and with a prohibition on the acceptance of any more than that fixed rent. No longer is it possible to advertise a dwelling in a way that discriminates against someone with children or who is receiving any form of state benefits unless there are exceptional grounds to do so. And a new standalone provision means that landlords will have to give serious consideration to any request from a tenant to keep a pet.

Later in 2027, it is expected that the government will have established its new landlord database, which private landlords will be required to join as well as a new Housing Ombudsman scheme to consider tenant complaints. By

2035, a new Decent Homes Standard may require those private landlords who are still in the market to have invested in the improvement of their properties to the required standard.

All of this represents new challenges for private landlords, letting agents, legal professionals and tenant advisers.

Looking over their shoulders is a rigorous new enforcement regime that is no longer complaints-led and in which local housing authorities are incentivised to make full use of the financial penalties that are now available to them, as an alternative to prosecution and to be proactive in enforcement. Getting it wrong is going to be expensive. So what of the future?

If it was the Housing Act 1988 which opened up the modern residential lettings market as an investment opportunity, which anyone could join if they had the wealth and confidence to do so, it is the Renters' Rights Act 2025 which may lead to a professionalisation of that market, as small private landlords drop out when properties fall vacant. There may also be a resurgence of those avoidance mechanisms that fell into disuse at the end of the 1980s. Such avoidance mechanisms might include landlords making greater use of holiday lets or company lets which are outside the assured tenancy regime. Or alternatively choosing to let through an intermediary, such as a local authority or housing association, instead of directly to an occupational tenant. It would then be for that intermediary to shoulder those landlord responsibilities and guarantees a return of vacant possession at the end of the lease.

Amongst the winners could be a new breed of property investment company able to navigate the changes and buy up tenanted properties and provide an escape for anyone wanting to cut their losses and have nothing more to do with residential letting. Such companies already exist for homeowners in financial difficulties and whose properties are threatened with repossession.

This book only applies to the changes as they apply to the law in England. This point is significant as the 2025 Act also contains separate standalone sections covering the law in Scotland and Wales, which are not covered in this book. It is also structured in a way that introduces the Renters' Rights Act 2025 and what it means for anyone affected by the changes. An introductory chapter sets out the timeline for implementation of the Act, starting 1 May 2026 and ending 2035. The following chapter explains the fundamental changes brought about by the 2025 Act, including the abolition of Section 21 evictions as well as fixed-term tenancies and what it means for the parties involved.

The third chapter lists and explains the new grounds of possession on which any landlord must rely to recover possession of a property through the courts. Some of these new possession grounds are 'non-fault' and are intended to compensate for the withdrawal of the Section 21 eviction by enabling landlords to repossess when they can prove genuine reasons to do so. But possession can no longer be gained on a whim. Even when there are no changes in a substantive ground for possession, there will almost certainly be changes in the process of gaining possession, most significantly through longer lead-in periods. The fourth chapter explains the process of regaining possession of a property through the courts using one of the new statutory grounds and the hurdles that must first be circumvented. Subsequent chapters deal with a new landlord's duty to ensure that tenancies are properly documented, including a statutory requirement to notify existing tenants of their change in status and the new rights that are attached to their tenancies. Other landlord duties are then explained regarding non-discrimination and dealing with a tenant's request to keep a pet.

Later chapters explain the new enforcement regime and what a landlord and letting agent might do when threatened with a financial penalty. Councils have also now been granted aggressive investigation powers, which allow authorised housing officers to enter premises, ask questions, and seize documentation. The final chapters explain new registration requirements for landlords as well as the Decent Homes Standard, which will apply from 2035 and may require significant capital investment on private landlords to bring their properties up to standard.

Suggested acknowledgment

V.Charles Ward addresses in practical legal terms the effect of the changes and what landlords and their agents need to do to comply with the new law.

1 Preparing for change

The coming into force of the Renters' Rights Act 2025 ('the 2025 Act') on 1 May 2026 could take many thousands of private residential landlords unawares. It isn't that the UK government hasn't published guidance sheets for landlords; it is just that finding that information requires effort.

Many of those landlords will soon discover that they can no longer recover possession of their properties on a whim, but only if they can prove one of the new statutory grounds for evicting a tenant. In many cases, tenants who formerly could have been evicted on as little as two months notice are now 'sitting tenants' with lifetime security of tenure. That discovery may come about the first time that the landlord tries to increase the rent on an existing tenancy and learns that they have to follow a new statutory process. Just 'putting up the rent' is no longer an option.

Residential landlords must also be fully up to date with new documentary requirements for residential tenancies. A tenancy agreement is no longer what the landlord or letting agent decides to put in it. There are also new regulatory requirements governing the content of a tenancy agreement or Statement of Terms issued after 1 May 2026. Extra care may be required in drafting those tenancy terms to ensure that sufficient express reference is made to any special non-fault grounds on which that particular landlord may wish to rely to recover possession of a property, if they want to sell that property or occupy the property themselves or for members of their family.

For tenancies already existing on 1 May 2026, landlords must serve an 'Information Sheet' on those tenants in a prescribed format, which tells those existing tenants how the changes brought about by the Renters' Reform Act 2025 will affect them.

Landlords and letting agents who do not get documentation right at the outset could not only face significant financial penalties but may also inhibit their ability to regain possession of their properties, even when they might otherwise have good legal grounds for doing so. Landlords and letting agents may also face significant financial penalties if prospective lettings are not marketed in a way which is fully compliant with the terms of the 2025 Act.

DOI: 10.1201/9781003681403-1

Going forward, anything advertising a proposed letting (other than a 'To Let' Notice fixed to the property itself) will need to specify the exact rent at which the premises will be let and with a prohibition on any landlord or letting agent accepting more than the advertised rent. Whilst landlords can still agree to accept less than the advertised rent, any landlord tempted to overprice their property may find an incoming tenant applying to a tribunal for a rent reduction.

Care must also be taken to ensure that a new letting is not marketed in a way which unfairly discriminates against a family with children or someone receiving state benefits of any description. Whilst landlords can still take into account a prospective tenant's ability to pay the reserved rent, those financial calculations must ensure that income received from state benefits is not treated less favourably than other income.

Local housing authorities have always had statutory responsibilities for enforcing housing legislation, particularly when it comes to unlawful eviction and harassment. Those statutory housing responsibilities now extend across the whole spread of residential landlord legislation.

Going forward, enforcement of landlord legislation will no longer just be reactive and complaint-led. Instead, the government now expects local housing authorities to be aggressive and proactive in the enforcement of landlord legislation, using the full range of financial penalties and investigatory powers which have now been provided. These include new powers enabling councils to insist that landlords and letting agents answer questions, and with additional powers to enter premises and seize documentation, backed, if necessary, by a magistrate's warrant.

Councils are also expected to formulate detailed written policies for the investigation and enforcement of the new legislation. All of this creates a need for more professionalism when it comes to letting out residential property.

Whilst it must be expected that leading residential letting agencies will have fully updated their documentation and processes to prepare for the coming in the force of the 2025 Act, those landlords most likely to be caught out are those who choose to deal with matters themselves instead of using a reputable letting agent or at least obtaining the appropriate legal advice, if they want to save an agents' commission by letting out their properties directly.

Just as many landlords will be caught unaware, so will many tenants, particularly those who do not receive these statutory 'Information Sheet' or Statement of Terms and are therefore unaware of their rights.

What seems clear is that a new regime will take time to settle in. Expensive mistakes will be made. There will be many issues for judges to ponder. It must also be assumed that in the coming months, there will be market changes. For example:

1 Some landlords may take the opportunity to get out of the lettings market altogether if they have an opportunity to do so.

2 There may be a greater emphasis on avoidance by those landlords who wish to retain a rental income but without the responsibility of a sitting tenant. Options might include company or holiday lets or letting through an intermediary, such as a local authority or housing association.

Landlords who stay in the rental market (whether willingly or unwillingly) will also need to remember that the longer-term government objective is to bring all private rented accommodation up to the recently published Decent Homes Standard. Existing substandard properties will need to be improved to that standard by the current proposed 2035 implementation date.

Finally, it is worth mentioning that residential landlord legislation does not exist in isolation. Its workability is dependent on an efficient civil court system, which enables landlords to recover possession quickly when they have legitimate grounds to do so. At the moment, that doesn't seem to be happening.

Currently, median times from the issue of proceedings to obtaining judgement at a possession hearing are up to ten weeks (possibly longer in London). If the tenant then refuses to move on the possession date, up to a further 34-week delay to get a bailiff appointment is added to the longer lead-in periods.

A landlord relying on the mandatory Ground 8 has to wait until the rent is at least 13 weeks in arrears before they can even start to serve a Section 8 notice claiming possession on that specific ground. That Section 8 notice would then need to give a four-week lead-in period before possession proceedings can be started in the county court (at week 18), perhaps then a further ten weeks before the case comes onto hearing (week 28). And if a possession order is made but the tenant refuses to vacate, a further, say, 30 weeks to get a bailiff's appointment (week 58) can be added. In other words, there is an eviction process which could take up to a year to complete, even when the tenant remains in serious arrears. And that's assuming that the case does not have to be adjourned, either because of administrative delays or because the landlord's right to possession is being challenged.

This book aims to provide private landlords, letting agents and anyone else involved in the residential lettings market with a ready source of reference to the changes brought out by the Renters' Rights Act 2025 on 1 May 2026 as well as later changes which will take effect on dates to be announced. We have referred throughout this book to the Renters' Rights Act 2025 simply as the 2025 Act.

Because the 2025 Act is UK-wide legislation which covers Scotland as well as Wales, this book only covers the law as existing in England on 1 May 2026. Those 1 May 2026 changes will primarily affect private residential landlords and letting agents. The 2025 Act will not apply to registered social landlords until a date in 2027, which at the time of writing is yet to be specified. Those registered social landlords will also be less affected by the changes, as many social tenancies are already lifetime assured. What this means is that until the 2025 Act is extended to registered social landlords, there will be two statutory regimes for residential letting, which run side by side.

It is only private landlords (as opposed to registered social landlords) who, from 1 May 2026, are directly affected by the abolition of Section 21 evictions – the automatic conversion of fixed-term tenancies into assured periodic tenancies and the new tenant rights conferred by the 2025 Act, which is set out in the following chapters of this book. However, the difference may not be so marked as many social landlords already opt to give their tenants lifetime security of tenure. So for the time being, the differences between private landlords and social landlords are mainly differences as to process. Until the 2025 Act is extended to social lettings, the Housing Act 1988 will continue to apply to social lettings as it did before 1 May 2026. So for social lettings, there is no immediate change from the law as it existed before 1 May 2026.

Note that Section 145(5) of the 2025 Act defines a 'social housing assured tenancy' as an assured tenancy of social housing within the meaning of Part 2 of the Housing and Regeneration Act 2008, where the landlord is a private registered provider of social housing. As will be seen in Chapter 3, setting out the new Section 8 Grounds of possession, registered housing associations are classed as 'private registered providers', to distinguish them from public sector landlords, even though most housing associations are themselves 'not for profit'.

The 2025 Act received Royal Assent on 25 October 2025 and represents the most far-reaching reform of private residential tenancy legislation since the Thatcher Government's Housing Act 1988 ('the 1988 Act'), opened up the private rented market and introduced the modern legislative framework for private residential lettings.

The primary purpose of the 2025 Act is not to abolish and replace the modern statutory framework for private residential lettings as set out in the 1988 Act. That basic structural framework remains substantially intact, as is the 1988 legislation itself but in its amended form. What the 2025 Act seeks to do instead is to rebalance the legal relationship between private residential landlords and their tenants, so that existing tenants can no longer be threatened with eviction when faced with a rent increase or their ability to complain about premises being no longer fit for habitation. It is also intended to create a fairer market for prospective tenants by outlawing discrimination against families with children as well as those in receipt of government benefits.

For landlords, the issue is the complexity of the new legislation and the fact that much of it will operate retrospectively, in particular, as regards the abolition of the old assured shorthold tenancies which hitherto had formed the bulk of the private residential lettings market.

Going forward, the assumption is that any private residential tenant occupying premises on 1 May 2026 may continue to occupy those premises for as long as they want to or at least until the landlord is able to prove one of the statutory grounds for obtaining possession (which do not all require proof of fault on the part of the tenant). There are also transitional provisions which temporarily protect residential landlords who had already initiated possession proceedings before the core provisions of the Act took effect on 1 May 2026. But these transitional protections are limited and will not protect any landlord who has not filed possession proceedings in the county court before the cut-off date of 1st August 2026.

Because the Renters' Rights Act 2025 received Royal Assent as recently as 27 October 2025, private residential landlords have only had six months to get ready for the implementation of its main reforms on 1 May 2026. These reforms involve not only the abolition of the old assured shorthold tenancies and their replacement by lifetime tenancies but also the restructuring of existing residential tenancy agreements, which can now only run from month to month instead of locking tenants into a fixed minimum term. Henceforth, these tenancies will be known as 'assured periodic tenancies' and the changes will operate retrospectively. These changes are also accompanied by a raft of new landlord duties, which will include the need to serve notices on existing tenants, which explain how the statutory changes will affect their tenancies. At the same time, those same landlords will also need to update template tenancy agreements to ensure that new tenancies created after 1 May 2026 are fully compliant with the 2025 Act.

To complicate matters further, the 2025 Act will not apply equally to the whole of the private residential rented sector. There are exceptions in the 2025 Act legislation for housing association lettings as well as lettings related to the carrying out by a local authority of its homelessness duties under the Housing Act 1996. It means that for the time being, those registered social landlords will be in a halfway house, with some aspects of the legislation applying from, 1st May 2026, but other parts, including restrictions against accepting advance rent and rental deposits, will be postponed to a later date.

Going forward, the cost of getting it wrong will be expensive for any private residential landlord still remaining in the market after 1 May 2026. Some of those landlords will have no choice about remaining in the market, as existing residential tenancies would have already converted to lifetime assured periodic tenancies. To make the legislation easier to enforce, local housing authorities have been given extensive powers to impose discretionary financial penalties from £5,000 to £40,000 for even the smallest technical breach. And don't expect any second chances.

The government has published a series of guidance notes (both statutory and non-statutory) to help landlords, letting agents as well as local housing authorities to understand this mass of complex legislation.

The key changes

The key changes brought about by the 2025 Act can be summarised as follows:

*__The abolition of Section 21 of the Housing Act 1988__, which gave a landlord the right to end an assured shorthold tenancy on giving as little as two months prior written notice in the prescribed form. Provided the landlord followed the correct process, the court had no discretion to refuse a possession order, and the tenant would be evicted. An accelerated possession procedure also enabled a landlord, using Section 21, to obtain a possession order against the former tenant without the need for a court hearing. What has changed with effect from 1 May 2026 is the abolition of assured shorthold tenancies (with retrospective effect) and removing along with it, the ability of landlords to evict tenants without cause under Section 21 of the 1988 Act. Such shorthold tenancies as existed before 1 May 2026 are now converted by statute into assured periodic tenancies, conferring lifetime security tenure. But the abolition of Section 21 does not mean the end of no-fault evictions, as landlords will still have a statutory right to evict a tenant if they require use of the premises for their own occupation or for their family, or if they can demonstrate a genuine intention to sell the property with vacant possession. Where landlords had already served a valid Section 21 notice in sufficient time before the new law took effect on 1 May 2026, transitional provisions will preserve their right to evict under that section notice, if they are able to issue possession proceedings in the county court before the 1 August 2026 cut off, failing which the earlier Section 21 notice will lapse.

*__The abolition of fixed-term residential tenancies__. It is no longer possible for a landlord to lock their tenant into a fixed-term residential tenancy from which the tenant cannot escape. After 1 May 2026, existing fixed-term assured tenancies converted automatically to month-to-month assured periodic tenancies which a tenant can end at any time by giving two months prior written notice to their landlord. But landlords cannot unilaterally end an assured periodic tenancy except by proving one of the amended statutory grounds.

*__A regulated process for increasing rents__. The repeal of Section 21 evictions means that a landlord can no longer use the threat of eviction to demand an increase in rent. Going forward, the only way in which a landlord will be able to impose a rental increase on an assured tenant is either by mutual agreement or through the statutory process, as contained in Section 13 of the 1988 Act (as amended by the 2025 Act).

*__All assured residential tenancies must now be in writing__. The 2025 Act imposes a new obligation on a landlord to issue written tenancy terms, whether or not contained within a conventional tenancy agreement. There is also a new regulation as to the content of those written tenancy terms. For tenancy agreements already in existence before 1 May 2026, there is a requirement on landlords to serve on their tenants a statutory notice, explaining the effect of the changes to their tenancy terms.

***Changes to the grounds for possession**. The 2025 Act makes extensive changes to the grounds for possession contained in Schedule 2 of the Housing Act 1988 and how a landlord can use those grounds for possession. Some of those changes compensate for the abolition of the Section 21 eviction, by giving a landlord an express right to evict in circumstances where they have a genuine intention to sell the property or occupy it for their own purposes or for other members of their family. But what is different from Section 21 is that any landlord placing reliance on any of these new mandatory non-fault grounds must prove their case to a County Court judge, and there is at least a 12-month moratorium on re-letting, where a previous tenant has been evicted on those new mandatory grounds. Other 2025 Act changes extend the lead-in period before a landlord can trigger particular grounds for possession. For example, a landlord's right to recover possession on the grounds that rent was at least two months in arrears has now been extended to three months arrears. There are also extensions to the time a landlord needs to give, when relying on particular fault or non-fault-based grounds for possession. When seeking possession on grounds of rent arrears, landlords must also now take account of benefit payments confirmed as due to the defaulting tenant but which have not yet been received by that tenant. For ease of reference, we have referred to these extended notices in the section describing these new grounds of possession:

***Protection from Discrimination.** A landlord can no longer discriminate against a prospective tenant who is in receipt of benefits or will have children living with them or visiting them. Other forms of discrimination (e.g. on grounds of race, sex or disability) had previously been outlawed by the Equality Act 2010.

***Keeping a pet**. The 2025 Act does not give a tenant an absolute right to keep a pet but enables them to ask their landlord for permission to keep a particular pet and for that request to be given reasonable consideration.

***The creation of new offences and financial penalties**. The Act now makes it illegal for a landlord to 'bluff' a tenant into vacating premises by pretending to rely on grounds for possession which they do not believe can be substantiated in law. The Act also gives local housing authorities an increased regulatory role, which includes the imposition of financial penalties as well as prosecution. The Act also makes it easier for tenants to obtain redress by applying to a Housing Ombudsman.

***Abolition of Bidding Wars.** The Act abolishes the ability of landlords to force prospective tenants to bid against each other for a particular property.

Assured agricultural occupancies

Although the 2025 Act is primarily concerned with the private residential lettings market, there is another type of tenancy for which it makes special provision, known as the assured agricultural occupancy.

Before 1976, an agricultural tenant occupying service accommodation provided by their employer could be evicted immediately once their employment had ended. This changed with the Rent Agriculture Act 1976, which conferred lifetime security of tenure on those former agricultural employees, at least until suitable alternative accommodation could be provided. These changes were also accommodated within Sections 24, 25 and Schedule 3 of the 1988 Act.

Historically, these agricultural lettings always provided better protections for a current or former tenant, as the protections against eviction would still apply even if the original tenancy had been granted at a very low or zero rent. Post-15 January 1989, an agricultural landlord had the option of granting a new employee an assured shorthold tenancy as an alternative to granting a fully assured agricultural occupancy. However, with the post-1 May 2026 abolition of assured short holds, the position has further changed.

To compensate for the abolition of the alternative of a shorthold tenancy, Section 24(3) of the 2025 Act now inserts an opting out provision in the form of a new Section 24A of the 1988 Act. This opt-out will enable an agricultural landlord to serve an 'opt-out notice' on a prospective agricultural tenant before that tenancy is entered into and only so long as it is not a continuation of an existing agricultural occupancy. That notice would have to be in a format prescribed by regulations. The effect of that opt-out notice will be that the tenancy will be a regular assured periodic tenancy, as long as other qualifying criteria are met for it to be an assured tenancy.

The primary feature of an agricultural occupancy is that a former agricultural tenant is not required to vacate on termination of their employment, even if it is the tenant who had terminated their own employment. Other statutory grounds for possession will then apply as they do for other assured tenancies, save that some of these statutory grounds for possession, involving termination of a superior lease or tenancy, cannot be relied on by landlords to terminate an agricultural occupancy. However, the provision of suitable alternative accommodation will always enable termination of an existing agricultural occupancy if the landlord urgently requires the premises to house another agricultural worker. In those circumstances, the landlord can ask the local housing authority to rehouse a former agricultural tenant so as to free up that property for another employee. To qualify as an agricultural worker within the meaning of the Rent Agriculture Act 1976, that person must have worked in agriculture for at least 91 out of the previous 104 weeks, with allowance being made for any illness or injury preventing that person from being at work. Where the agricultural dwelling was originally let on a zero or very low rent, any landlord wishing to increase the rent will have to go through the statutory process set out on Section 13 of the Housing Act 1988 as amended. Note that the tenancy cannot be regarded as an assured agricultural occupancy if it is protected under other legislation, such as the Agricultural Holdings Act1986 or the Agricultural Tenancies Act 1995. It is important to note that the difference between an assured agricultural occupancy and a regular assured periodic tenancy is now much less marked as both potentially grant lifetime security of tenure and it is for agricultural landlords to take their own employment advice on which is to be preferred on a new letting.

Timeline

Although the Renters' Rights Act 2025 received Royal Assent on 25 October 2025, its provisions are being brought into force in phases. The first part of the Act came into force on 27 December 2025, giving local housing authorities (being district and unitary councils) new powers to investigate breaches of 'landlord legislation', not only under the 2025 Act, but also including Sections 1 and 1A of the Protection from Eviction Act 1977, Chapter 1 of Part 1 of the Housing Act 1988, Sections 83(1) and 84(1) of the Enterprise and Regulatory Reform Act 2013 and Sections 21 to 23 of the Housing and Planning Act 2016. However, the main provisions of the 2025 Act will take effect in three phases, with the first tranche of reforms taking effect on 1 May 2026 and with the remaining stages taking effect later this year and in 2027, when it will also be rolled out to housing associations.

In preparation for the staged implementation of the Act, The Ministry of Housing, Communities and Local Government (MHCLG) has and will be publishing a raft of regulations and official guidance to supplement the provisions of the Act.

On 13 November 2025, the MHCLG published its timetable for implementing the 2025 Act in its policy paper titled 'Implementing the Renters' Rights Act 2025: Our Roadmap for Reforming the Private Rented Sector'. Here is a summary of that timetable.

Phase 1 (1 May 2026)

- Abolition of Section 21 'no-fault' evictions.
- Introduction of assured periodic tenancies in place of fixed-term assured tenancies, which will mean that tenants can stay in their property as long as they want to or until a landlord serves a valid Section 8 notice. Tenants will be able to end their tenancy at any time by giving two months notice to the landlord.
- Reforms to the grounds for possession for terminating assured periodic tenancies.
- Rental increases will only be permitted annually and in accordance with the revised procedure contained in Section 13 of the 1988 Act, giving a tenant at least two months prior written notice of a proposed rent increase before it can take effect.

- A ban on rental bidding and accepting more than one month's advance rent.
- Prohibiting discrimination against renters who have children or receive benefits.
- Requiring landlords to consider tenant requests to keep a pet.
- Strengthening local council enforcement and rent repayment orders – with greater use of civil penalties.

Note that the abolition of Section 21 evictions and other tenancy reforms during Phase 1 will not apply initially to the social rented sector, which happens during the second phase of implementation.

Phase 2 (Late 2026 or 2027)

During the second tier of changes, which are expected to take effect later in 2026 or in 2027, the MHCLG intends to introduce the Private Rented Sector (PRS) Database and PRS Landlord Ombudsman. The database will be rolled out regionally and it will be mandatory for landlords to sign up for it and pay an annual fee. Regulations will state the information, which is required for each registration, which will include, as a minimum:

- The landlord's contact details
- Property details, including the full address, type of property, number of bedrooms, number of households/residents and whether the property is let furnished
- Safety information – gas, electric and energy performance certificates.

During Phase 2, the MHCLG will also establish the PRS Landlord Ombudsman to provide a redress service when things go wrong. It will also provide tools, guidance and training to landlords on handling tenant complaints. This Ombudsman scheme will be mandatory for PRS landlords, who will be required to fund the service. However, implementation of the Ombudsman scheme will not happen until after the introduction of the database. The Ombudsman scheme is expected to take up to 18 months from implementation to set up.

Phase 3: A new decent homes standard in the private rented sector

Implementation of these later provisions of the 2025 Act is expected to be longer term and will ensure that all PRS properties meet a minimum standard of housing quality and provide local councils with the powers they need to take enforcement action where those standards are not being met. It is suggested that these revisions may be brought into force in either 2035 or 2037.

When does the Renters' Rights Act 2025 apply?

The Renters' Rights Act 2025 can only apply where there is a 'tenancy' as opposed to some other residential occupancy arrangement. An example of the latter might be someone who occupies residential accommodation as a lodger or as a paying guest in someone else's home. A lodger can be evicted at any time on reasonable notice from the householder. A residential tenancy can only exist in law when there is 'exclusive possession', that is to say, the right of that tenant to their own private space. The key legal reference point to determine whether occupation of residential accommodation can truly be regarded as a tenancy is the landmark case of *Street v Mountford {1985} UKHL4,* when the House of Lords had to decide whether a two-room occupancy arrangement, labelled as a 'Licence', was in fact a Rent Act protected tenancy. The Lawlords said that it was fully protected under the Rent Act 1977 and for the following reasons:

- It is necessary to look at the substance of the arrangement, not how the parties chose to label it.
- The first ingredient of a 'tenancy' was the exclusive possession, which meant the tenant's right to exclude anyone else, including the landlord, from the accommodation, save for specific purposes, such as repairs.
- The second ingredient of a tenancy was that it had to be for a term, whether it is expressed as a fixed term or as a periodic term, such as a weekly or monthly tenancy.
- There has to be a rental element, which would exclude any gratuitous arrangement.

Although the 2025 Act makes reference to some types of agricultural tenancies (as well as earlier Rent Act lettings), it is primarily only concerned with the private rented sector (PRS) and those particular residential tenancies which fall within the category of 'assured tenancies' as defined later. The distinction is important as there are other types of residential tenancy which are not 'assured', either because they are covered by some other statutory lettings regime, such as local authority lettings under the Housing Act 1985, or otherwise because they are specifically excluded from being assured tenancies.

2 The fundamentals

In this chapter, we look at key structural changes to the system of residential letting in England, which took effect on 1 May 2026 as a result of the implementation of the first significant stage of the Renters' Rights Act 2025. We look not only at the abolition of the old Section 21 evictions but also how the legal relationship between residential landlords and tenants has changed on that date and with retrospective effect. In the following chapter, we look more closely at the new and amended grounds of possession which took effect on 1 May 2026 and the extended lead-in times between the date a landlord can serve a Section 8 notice of seeking possession and the date possession proceedings can actually be implemented in the county court. We also look at the new rules to which a landlord or prospective landlord (as well as letting agents) must adhere when letting residential premises after 1 May 2026 and the consequences of getting it wrong. These include new rules on documenting a new residential tenancy, particularly if, sometime in the future, the landlord may wish to sell the property with vacant possession or use the property for their own occupation or for that of a close family member. We also look at new rules for landlords and letting agents when marketing premises for let. These new rules will prevent direct or indirect discrimination against respective tenants with children or who are receiving state benefits of any description. Where properties are advertised for let, the advertisement must state clearly the rent which used to be charged, and any form of competitive bidding between tenants is outlawed.

What is an assured periodic tenancy?

The definition of an 'assured tenancy' remains as set out in Section 1 of the Housing Act 1988 as supplemented by Schedule 1 of that Act (lettings which cannot be assured tenancies). In summary, an assured tenancy remains a residential tenancy in which:

- The tenant is an individual [which excludes company lets].
- The tenant occupies the premises as their only or principal home (which therefore excludes someone who takes a tenancy of residential premises

DOI: 10.1201/9781003681403-2

primarily for occupation by someone else who is not part of their household or who takes multiple residential tenancies, save the one which they occupy as their only or principal home).

- Residential tenancies which are excluded from being assured tenancies because they are listed in Schedule 1 of the 1988 Act. Exceptions include residential tenancies at a very high or low rent, student lettings, resident landlord lettings, or lettings which are covered by other regulatory regimes, such as local authority secure tenancies granted under the Housing Act 1985). **Note** that by Section 31(1) of the 2025 Act, the list of excluded tenancies now prevents any fixed-term lease of more than 21 years from becoming an assured tenancy. This exclusion tidies up the law, and now means that a long residential lease cannot accidentally be brought into the assured tenancy regime because of a high annual ground rent (£1,000 in Greater London or £250 elsewhere), with the associated threat of eviction if that rent falls more than three months in arrears. Fixed-term leases of between 7 and 21 years granted before 1 May 2026 are also excluded from becoming assured tenancies.

Knowing what constitutes of an 'assured tenancy' is important as the Renters' Rights Act 2025 only covers tenancies which were either originally granted as or have since become residential assured tenancies. It is also apparent from the statutory definition that a tenancy which was assured at the outset may cease to remain an assured tenancy if the tenant ceases to occupy it as their only or principal home.

On 13 November 2025, the MHCLG issued 'Renting Out Your Property: Guidance for Landlords and Letting Agents – Tenancy Types'. It explains in plain language the different types of residential tenancy and, more importantly, which tenancies are regarded as assured periodic tenancies within the meaning of the 2025 Act. It states that, from 1 May 2026, a residential letting granted by a private residential landlord can only be an assured periodic tenancy if all of the following criteria apply:

- The landlord does not live at the property.
- The property is the tenant's main accommodation.
- Tenants have their own room, but might share a bathroom or kitchen with other tenants.

The same guidance also explains that a residential tenancy cannot be an assured periodic tenancy if any of the following applies:

- The landlord lives at the property.
- The property is purpose-built student accommodation and the tenants are university students and the landlord has signed up to the National Code. Note that the National Code refers to the ANUK/Unipol Code of

Standards, a voluntary scheme that private and university providers join to prove that their housing meets high standards and which guarantees safe building conditions, clear repair timescales, professional management and a formal complaints process.
- The tenancy has a fixed term of more than 21 years (see above).
- The rent is more than £100,000 a year.
- The rent is less than £250 a year (or less than £1,000 in London).
- It is a business tenancy or tenancy of licensed premises (which will be covered by other tenancy legislation).
- It is a holiday let.

Note: That the immediate implications of the tenancy not being an assured periodic tenancy are as follows:

- The tenant will not have lifetime security of tenure, unless equivalent security is already provided under other legislation, such as the Rent Act 1977 or Agricultural Holdings Act 1986.
- There will be no automatic conversion of a fixed-term tenancy into an assured periodic tenancy.
- The rules relating to the issuing of a Statement of Terms or Statutory Information Sheet for existing tenancies will not apply.
- The rules against discrimination against families or benefit claimants will not apply.
- The landlord is under no obligation to give reasonable consideration to a tenant's request to keep a pet.
- The landlord is not required to prove any of the statutory Schedule 2 Grounds to evict the tenant but will in many cases, still be required under the Protection of Eviction Act 1977 to obtain a court order for possession before evicting, following due process.

In relation to 'assured agricultural tenancies or occupancies', the MHCLG Guidance advises that the tenant needs to have worked in agriculture for 91 of the previous 104 weeks for at least 34 hours a week unless a work-related injury or disease prevented full-time work and to have had exclusive occupation of a separate dwelling under a tenancy or licence provided or arranged by the employer. In those circumstances, it doesn't matter that the tenant is required to pay little or no rent under the tenancy or license agreement. However, before that tenancy starts, a landlord may give the tenant statutory notice that the tenancy will not be an assured agricultural occupancy.

The abolition of fixed-term tenancies, Section 21 evictions, and assured shortholds

Before 1 May 2026, an assured tenancy, including one of the old assured shorthold tenancies, could be granted either for a fixed term or periodically, say from month to month. It was also usual practice for a landlord to grant a residential tenancy for an initial term of, say, 6 or 12 months, which would then automatically continue beyond its term date as a periodic tenancy unless terminated by formal written notice given by the landlord at least two months before the term date or at any time thereafter. A tenant was not required to give any formal advance written notice to their landlord if they intended to leave at the end of the initial fixed term but they would be required to give at least a month's notice of their intention to vacate if the initial fixed-term tenancy had already ended but they remained in possession of the premises.

For the tenant, an initial fixed term of 6 or 12 months meant that, so long as they kept to the terms of their tenancy, they could not be evicted before the end of their contractual term. It also meant that they were locked into their tenancy for its full contractual minimum term, even if they wanted to move elsewhere.

Section 1 of the 2025 Act has now abolished, with retrospective effect, the creation of fixed-term assured tenancies. Such fixed-term tenancies as formerly existed before 1 May 2026 have been converted by statute into monthly periodic tenancies which continue indefinitely until terminated. In each case, the period of the tenancy must equate to the intervals in which rental payments fall due. So an existing residential tenancy which provides for rent to be paid on the first day of each month will become a monthly tenancy which is automatically renewable on the first day of each subsequent month. Likewise, rental payments falling due on a 28-day cycle will become a tenancy which renews every 28 days.

Whilst there is nothing to prevent a landlord creating a new periodic tenancy for less than a 28-day cycle, say from week to week, it is no longer possible for a landlord to create a tenancy for a fixed term longer than one month. The default rental conversion formula for calculating the new monthly rent for former fixed-term residential tenancies converted by operation of law into periodic tenancies is stated by Section 1(5) of the 2025 Act to be:

$$\frac{R}{D} \times 30.42$$

'R' is the rent which would otherwise have been due for the first rent-period.
'D' is the number of whole days in that period.

The abolition of fixed-term assured tenancies with retrospective effect means that a residential tenant can now end their assured tenancy at any time by giving the landlord at least two months prior written notice in accordance with new Subsection 5 of the Protection from Eviction Act 1977, as introduced by Section 21 of the 2025 Act. It does not matter that the tenant may have originally contracted for a longer fixed term. **Note** also the following:

- Once given, a tenant's notice to quit cannot be withdrawn except by written agreement with the landlord.
- On the issue of a valid notice to quit, the assured tenancy will automatically end, and the landlord will be able to apply immediately to a court for the order for possession if the tenant has not previously vacated in accordance with their notice.

- Failure to give a valid notice to quit means that, even after they have vacated the property, that tenant may still be contractually liable to make rental payments until the tenancy is properly terminated.
- That even when a compliant tenant's notice to quit has been given, the tenancy cannot end until the expiry of the current period of the tenancy, namely the first rent payment after the minimum two-month notice period. It is therefore important that a tenant's notice to quit is given in the correct, legally binding format.
- There is nothing to prevent a landlord from agreeing to accept termination on less than two months prior written notice, whether or not the tenancy agreement provides for this.
- Any contractual provision requiring the outgoing tenant to provide a longer period of notice or to provide that notice in a particular way has no legal effect.
- A tenant's notice to quit given by only one of multiple joint tenants will suffice to end the tenancy for all the joint tenants and will bind all other co-tenants.

Finally, note Section 10 of the 2025 Act which inserts a new Section 14ZC into the 1988 Act, which confirms an outgoing tenant's right to repayment of any advance rent relating to any days falling after the end of the tenancy and which does not affect any other entitlement to payment arising at the end of an assured tenancy.

3 The new grounds for possession

Although a key purpose of the Renters' Rights Act 2025 is to remove Section 21 no-fault evictions and thereby give residential tenants lifetime security tenure, other grounds for eviction remain but with modifications to adjust the balance of power in favour of residential tenants.

Some of these remaining grounds of possession have always required proof of fault on the part of the tenant, whilst other grounds of possession enable the landlord to regain possession without proof of any fault on the tenant's part. But these remaining non-fault grounds differ from the old Section 21 non-fault eviction, in that they are not entirely process driven. A landlord relying on one of these non-fault grounds to recover possession still has to prove their case. There is also a difference between those statutory grounds which give a judge a discretion of whether or not to grant a possession order, and if so on what terms, and those mandatory grounds of possession which give that judge no ability to refuse or delay the granting of a possession order. The mandatory grounds for possession are in Part I of the amended Schedule 2 of the 1988 Act and are the grounds on which a judge has no discretion to refuse a possession order once a landlord has proved their case. Part II of the amended Schedule 2 lists out those discretionary grounds for possession in which a judge is only obliged to grant a possession order when it is considered reasonable to do so.

The new mandatory grounds for possession

Ground 1 (as substituted by the 2025 Act) – premises required for occupation by landlord or family

This substituted ground for possession will apply if the current tenancy began at least one year before the expiry of the Section 8 notice of termination, and the landlord seeking possession requires the dwelling as their only or principal home or as a home for any of the landlord's immediate family. As substituted, this ground for possession is wider than the earlier Ground 1, as there

DOI: 10.1201/9781003681403-3

is no longer any requirement for the landlord to have previously occupied the dwelling as their only or principal home.

Note that a landlord who succeeds in recovering possession on this mandatory Ground 1 (or mandatory Ground 1A – see below) cannot within the 'restricted period' re-let the premises other than on a lease for at least 21 years or allow someone else to occupy on license in return for payment. For this purpose and elsewhere in the legislation, the 'restricted period' is defined by Section [16E(4)] to the 1998 Act, as inserted by Section 13 of the 2025 Act to mean the period *starting* with the date of service of the landlord's notice of termination and *ending* on the later of 12 months from the date possession is required under the notice or 12 months from the earliest date on which possession proceedings will begin. A new Section 16F to the 1998 Act provides an exception for a re-letting of the premises to someone within their immediate family as well as an exception for the grant of an occupational licence to someone who has contracted to purchase the property.

The restriction on re-letting within the restricted period also prevents the premises from being marketed for re-letting during that time. The restriction on advertising or marketing applies not only to the landlord but to anyone else engaged in letting agency work, but does not penalise anyone whose business involves only the placing of advertisements and who is not the landlord or someone engaged as a letting agent. **Note** that any breach of this restriction against re-letting during the restricted period is made a criminal offence by new Section 16J(2) of the 1998 Act and with the local housing authority being given a new Section 16K discretion to impose a civil penalty of up to £40,000 as an alternative to prosecution.

Note: Any landlord proposing to seek possession of premises under this mandatory Ground 1 must issue a Section 8 notice (see below) giving the tenant at least four months notice of the landlord's intention to recover possession on this non-fault ground.

Ground 1A – New ground for sale of dwelling house

This new mandatory possession Ground 1A entitles a landlord to end an assured tenancy if they intend to sell a freehold or a long leasehold interest in the premises and so long as the assured tenancy did not come into being by virtue of any of the provisions of Schedule 1 to the Rent Act 1977 or Section 4 of the Rent (Agriculture) Act 1976 [succession tenancies]. There are also the following additional qualifying criteria before a landlord can rely on this ground for possession, which is listed below:

i *Either* the current tenancy began at least one year before the expiry of the notice of termination *or* the premises are the subject of a compulsory purchase order and the landlord intends to sell their interest to the acquiring authority.

ii The landlord is *not* a registered provider of social housing.

Note that the same restrictions on relating or marketing for re-letting during the restricted period (see above) also applies to circumstances where possession is obtained on this Ground 1A

Note: Any landlord proposing to seek possession of premises under this mandatory Ground 1A must issue a Section 8 notice (see below) giving the tenant at least four months notice of the landlord's intention to recover possession on this non-fault ground. A landlord may also be prevented from relying on this Ground 1 if, at the outset of the tenancy, the landlord has not provided the tenant with a statement to the effect of the landlord's wish to regain possession under this Ground 1A

Ground 1B – New ground for possession after rent-to buy agreement (mandatory ground for possession)

This new ground for possession entitles a private registered provider of social housing who has let premises on an assured tenancy pursuant to a rent-to-buy agreement to recover possession if they intend any of the following:

i To sell a freehold or leasehold interest in the dwelling.
ii To grant a new lease for a fixed term of more than 21 years which cannot be terminated earlier by notice given by either party.
iii To grant an assured tenancy to another person pursuant to a rent-to-buy agreement.

The other qualifying criteria for use of this ground of possession are that the term of the rent-to-buy agreement has expired and the landlord seeking possession has complied with any provision in the rent-to-buy agreement requiring the landlord to offer the dwelling for sale to the tenant as well as any other contractual requirements relating to such offer. For the purposes of Ground 1B, a rent-to-buy agreement means a written agreement allowing the tenant to pay a rent no higher than 80% of market rent (including any service charge) and which gives notice that after the period stated in the agreement (not being less than ten years in Greater London or five years elsewhere), that the landlord intends to offer the dwelling for sale to the tenant.

Note that this ground for possession is only available to private registered providers of social housing, which is defined as an organisation operating in England which provides low-cost rental accommodation and/or low-cost home ownership options and which is registered with the Regulator of Social

Housing. The definition is wide enough to cover housing associations, charities as well as social landlords which operate for profit. The definition does not include local authority landlords.

Note also that any landlord reserving the right to seek possession on this special Ground 1B may be prevented from doing so unless, when first granting the tenancy, the landlord had included in the tenancy agreement or other Statement of Terms, a reservation to that effect (see Section 16D(3) and 16E(1)(f)). This restriction also applies to any application for possession using this special ground. The landlord's Section 8 notice seeking possession must give the tenant at least four months notice before the landlord can apply to the court for possession.

Mandatory Ground 2 – Sale by mortgagee – as amended by the 2025 Act

This ground for possession applies where the dwelling is subject to a mortgage and the mortgagee is entitled to exercise a power of sale in respect to the property and requires possession to enable it to sell with vacant possession. **Note** that the 2025 Act deleted the earlier requirement that the mortgage was in place before the beginning of the tenancy and that the tenant had previously been given notice that possession might be required under this ground. **Note** that the Landlord's Section 8 notice triggering the landlord's right to possession on this ground must give the tenant at least four months notice.

Mandatory ground 2ZA – New ground for possession where a superior lease ends (introduced by the 2025 Act) (social lettings only)

This new ground for possession gives certain categories of landlord who hold a leasehold interest under a superior lease which has either been terminated by the superior landlord on notice or is a fixed term tenancy scheduled to expire within 12 months, the ability to terminate the immediate tenancy. The only landlord of an assured tenancy to which this ground of possession can apply is any of the following:

- i A private registered provider of social housing (which includes a housing association)
- ii A landlord which is itself a tenant of a superior landlord under an agricultural tenancy within the meaning of the Agricultural Holdings Act 1986 or a farm business tenancy within the meaning of the Agricultural Tenancies Act 1995
- iii A landlord who held the dwelling for the purpose of making it available as supported accommodation

iv A company in which a local authority owns at least 50% of the issued share capital

Note that a Section 8 notice requiring possession on this Ground 2ZA must give the tenant at least four months notice. The landlord may also be prevented from relying on this ground if no statement was given to the tenant at the outset that possession may be required on this ground.

Note that this ground for possession does not apply to assured agricultural occupancies.

Mandatory Ground 2ZB – New ground for possession where a superior lease ends (introduced by the 2025 Act) (general)

This ground for possession applies where the immediate landlord holds its own interest in the dwelling under a fixed term lease of more than 21 years and which lease is due to expire within 12 months from the expiry of the notice from the immediate landlord to their occupational tenant, ending the assured tenancy. This ground will also apply in circumstances where the fixed-term lease has already continued beyond its term date, and any party to that superior lease has served a valid notice to determine the tenancy.

Note: That the principal difference between this general Ground 2ZB and the more restrictive Ground 2ZA above (which only applies to social landlords), is that this Ground 2ZB is only expressed to apply where the superior lease was originally granted for a fixed term of more than 21 years. The earlier Ground 2ZA can apply to a superior lease of any length.

Note that a Section 8 notice requiring possession on this Ground 2ZB must give the tenant at least four months notice. The landlord may also be prevented from relying on this ground if no statement was given to the tenant at the outset that possession may be required on this ground.

Note that this ground for possession does not apply to assured agricultural occupancies.

Mandatory Ground 2ZC – New ground for possession for superior landlord where superior lease has ended (general)

This ground for possession enables a *superior landlord* to recover possession against an assured tenant of the previous intermediate landlord whose intermediate lease had ended.

This ground of possession applies where, pursuant to Section 18 of the Housing Act 1988, an assured tenant has become the tenant of a superior landlord in circumstances where the intermediate landlord interest has come to an end.

In those circumstances, the superior landlord has six months, from the ending of the intermediate lease, to initiate possession proceedings against the assured tenant. However this ground for possession will only apply where the *intermediate landlord* had been a a private registered provider of social housing (see above); the tenant of a superior landlord under an agricultural tenancy or farm business tenancy; where the intermediate landlord provided supported living accommodation; or was a company in which a local authority owned at least 50% of the issued share capital.

Note that this particular ground of possession would cater for the situation where accommodation has been let by a private landlord to a registered provider of social housing, who then sublets to one of their own tenants. **Note** further that what makes this special Ground 2ZC different from the following general Ground 2ZD is that when qualifying circumstances apply, this Ground 2ZC will apply to intermediate tenancies shorter than 21 years.

Note that a Section 8 notice requiring possession on this Ground 2ZC must give the tenant at least four months notice. The landlord may also be prevented from relying on this ground if no statement was given to the tenant at the outset that possession may be required on this ground.

Note that this ground for possession does not apply to assured agricultural occupancies.

New mandatory Ground 2ZD. General right of superior landlord (having become the landlord pursuant to Section 18 of the Housing Act 1988) to bring an assured tenancy to an end following expiry of a long leasehold interest

This Ground 2ZD gives a superior landlord six months to initiate possession proceedings against an assured tenant following the termination of a fixed term intermediate residential lease (originally granted for a term of more than 21 years).

Note: Under Schedule 10 of the Local Government and Housing Act 1989 (which replaced Part 1 of the Landlord and Tenant Act 1954), a long residential lease will continue beyond its term date until terminated in accordance with the provisions of that Schedule 10. In those circumstances, the right of the superior landlord to recover possession from an assured tenant cannot then arise until the expired intermediate leasehold interest has been brought to an end by notice, when the superior landlord will have up to six months to initiate possession proceedings.

Note that a Section 8 notice requiring possession on this Ground 2ZD must give the tenant at least four months notice. The landlord may also be prevented from relying on this ground if no statement was given to the tenant at the outset that possession may be required on this ground.

Note that this ground for possession does not apply to assured agricultural occupancies.

Mandatory Ground 3 – Out of season letting of holiday accommodation

This former ground of possession has been deleted by the 2025 Act

Mandatory Ground 4 – Out-of-term lettings of student accommodation

This existing mandatory ground of possession covering out-of-term lettings of student accommodation is replaced by the following wording:

> *At some time within the period of 12 months ending with the beginning of the tenancy, the dwelling house was let on a tenancy falling within paragraph 8 of Schedule 1 [to the Housing Act 1988] and:*

If the tenancy arose by succession as mentioned in Section 39(5), notice was given to the previous tenant under Case 14 of Schedule 15 to the Rent Act 1977, and the tenancy is not an assured agricultural occupancy in respect of which the agricultural worker condition is fulfilled by virtue of Paragraph 3 of Schedule 3.

Note that Section 39(5) of the 1988 Act deals with succession tenancies under the Rent Act 1977 which have been converted to assured tenancies. Case 14 of Schedule 15 of the Rent Act 1977 also provided a mandatory ground for possession for out-of-term lettings of student accommodation where there had been previous student lettings by specified educational institutions, but only where the landlord of the out-of-term tenancy had previously given notice to the tenant that possession might be required on this ground. **Note** also that this ground of possession does not apply to student lettings by specified educational institutions, which are already prevented from becoming assured tenancies by Paragraph 8 of Schedule 1 of the 1988 Act (which continues unchanged). This Ground 4 instead applies to out-of-term lettings by any landlord (not just specified educational institutions) but only where the premises had previously been the subject of a student-letting by a specified educational institution within the preceding 12 months.

Specified educational institutions are defined by the *Assured and Protected Tenancies (Lettings to Students) Regulations 1998*, to include universities or university colleges as well as other publicly funded institutions providing further or higher education. The purpose of these regulations is to ensure that student accommodation provided by universities and other designated bodies can be easily managed by the institution without being subject to the full protection of an assured tenancy.

Note that a Section 8 notice served under this Ground 4 needs to only give the tenant two weeks notice before the landlord can commence possession proceedings. However, the Statement of Terms given to the tenant at the outset of the tenancy must have explained that the landlord may wish to obtain possession under this ground.

New Ground 4A – Possession of student accommodation for occupation by other students

This new mandatory ground of possession was introduced to compensate for the abolition of fixed-term student lettings. Under the new law, such tenancies can only be ended between 1 June and 30 September in any year to coincide with the ending of the academic year. Ground 4A entitles any landlord of any dwelling within an HMO (house in multiple occupation) to recover possession from a student in order to let the same premises to another student. To use this ground of possession, all of the following additional qualifying criteria must be met:

- Both the outgoing as well as the incoming students must meet the 'student test', which means that they must be attending a full-time course of a description mentioned in Schedule 6 Education Reform Act 1988 or associated Scottish or Northern Ireland legislation. A reasonable belief on the part of the landlord will suffice for these purposes.
- There can be no intervening tenancy to someone who does not satisfy the 'student test'.
- The landlord has previously given to the prospective tenant a written statement of the landlord's wish to be able to recover possession on this ground. But note that where a tenancy becomes an assured tenancy because of Paragraph 8(7) of Schedule 1 to the 1988 Act (as amended), it is sufficient that the written notice is given within 28 days of the tenancy becoming assured.
- The premises are an HMO or comprised within an HMO as defined by Section 254 of the Housing Act 2004, which applies where a single unit of accommodation is led to multiple persons who do not comprise a single household and who share some amenities.
- The interval between the student signing the tenancy agreement and the date the student actually takes possession of the dwelling is to be no more than six months.

A Section 8 notice specifying this Ground 4A must give the tenant at least four months notice before the landlord can apply for possession. **Note** also Section 8ZA of the 1988 Act (as introduced by Section 3(4) of the 2025 Act), which enables the court to dispense with the requirement that the student tenancy ended between 1 June and 30 September in any year, where it is just an equitable to do so.

Amended Ground 5 – Ministers of religion

This Ground 5 will apply where the dwelling is reserved for occupation by a minister of religion as a residence from which to perform their duties:

a [Requirement for advance notice now abolished by the 2025 Act]
b The court is satisfied that the dwelling is required for occupation by a minister of religion to perform their duties.
c If the tenancy arose by succession as mentioned in Section 39(5) [of the 1988 Act], notice was given to the previous tenant under Case 15 of Schedule 15 to the Rent Act 1977.
d The tenancy is not an assured agricultural occupancy in respect of which the agricultural worker condition is fulfilled by Paragraph 3 of Schedule 3 [of the 1988 Act].

A Section 8 notice specifying this ground must give the tenant at least two months notice before the landlord can apply to the court for a possession order. The landlord may also be prevented from relying on this ground if the Statement of Terms given to the prospective tenant at the outset did not specify that possession may be required on this ground.

New Ground 5A – Possession for occupation by agricultural worker

This ground of possession 5A applies where the landlord requires a dwelling to house a person who will be employed by that landlord in agriculture as a seasonal or permanent employee. 'Agriculture' is defined by Section 1 of the Rent Agriculture Act 1976 to cover livestock as well as arable farming, grazing and forestry.

A Section 8 notice specifying this Ground 5A must provide the tenant with at least two months notice before the landlord can apply to the county court for a possession order. Reference to the possibility of possession being required on this ground must also be contained in the Statement of Terms given to the prospective tenant at the outset.

New Ground 5B – Possession for occupation by a person who meets employment requirements

This new ground of possession applies only to private registered providers of social housing who let for the purpose of accommodating someone who meets requirements connected with their employment and who requires the dwelling to let it under a new tenancy to someone else who meets those requirements, and where the current tenant no longer fulfils those requirements. **Note** that this ground for possession enables registered social landlords to reserve accommodation for particular key workers. Where an incumbent tenant no longer meets the particular key worker specification, the landlord can then recover possession and re-let the property to someone else who does meet the key worker specification for that property. Note that there is no requirement for the tenant to be in a direct employment relationship with the RSL landlord.

A Section 8 notice specifying this Ground 5B must provide the tenant with at least two months notice before the landlord can apply to the county court for a possession order. Reference to the possibility of possession being required on this ground must also be contained in the Statement of Terms given to the prospective tenant at the outset.

New mandatory Ground 5(C) – Service accommodation

The old discretionary ground of possession 16 (service accommodation) has now become a new mandatory ground for possession and has been re-written in the following terms (summarised).

The new mandatory Ground 5C will apply where a dwelling was left to a tenant in consequence of their employment either by the landlord seeking possession or by a previous landlord under the same tenancy. This ground for possession will also apply to a letting previously granted pursuing to an agreement between the landlord and the tenant's employer. The right to possession is triggered either when the tenant has ceased to be in the relevant employment or in circumstances where the tenant was provided with temporary accommodation at the beginning of their employment and the same premises are now to be made available to another current or future employee.

A Section 8 notice specifying this Ground 5C must provide the tenant with at least two months notice before the landlord can apply to the county court for a possession order. Reference to the possibility of possession being required on this ground must also be contained in the Statement of Terms given to the prospective tenant at the outset. What makes this ground position different from Ground 5(B) above is that it is not restricted to registered social landlords, though there is a requirement that the landlord either employs the tenant directly or is in a contractual relationship with a third party who provides that accommodation on behalf of the landlord.

New mandatory ground for possession 5D for occupation as supported accommodation

This ground for possession applies where any landlord requires possession of a dwelling, to let it as supported accommodation in circumstances where that accommodation is held for the purpose of making it available for occupation as supported accommodation and the tenant did not enter into the tenancy for the purpose of receiving care, support or supervision.

A Section 8 notice specifying this Ground 5D must provide the tenant with at least two months notice before the landlord can apply to the county court for a possession order. Reference to the possibility of possession being required on this ground must also be contained in the Statement of Terms given to the prospective tenant at the outset.

New mandatory ground for possession 5E – Where premises let as supported accommodation

This new ground for possession applies where any landlord holds a dwelling for the purpose of making it available for occupation as supported accommodation, and the incumbent tenant did not enter the assured tenancy for the purpose of receiving care, support or supervision.

A Section 8 notice specifying this Ground 5E must provide the tenant with at least four weeks notice before the landlord can apply to the county court for a possession order. Reference to the possibility of possession being required on this ground must also be contained in the Statement of Terms given to the prospective tenant at the outset.

Mandatory ground for possession 5F – Where dwelling is occupied as supported accommodation

This new Ground 5F will enable any landlord to recover possession of supported accommodation where the continued provision of that support becomes unviable for any of the following reasons (summarised):

a The tenancy was granted to provide the tenant with support for a limited time to enable that tenant to live in other accommodation, and the need for that support has now ended.

b Someone other than the landlord provided support services to the tenant but that support has come to an end or that third party is not fulfilling their obligations to provide those services and, where the dwelling is not managed accommodation, the landlord has used reasonable endeavours to find alternative support provision but has not been able to do so.

c Where the accommodation or support was funded wholly or partly by a third party and that funding is no longer being provided or, where the dwelling is not managed accommodation, the landlord has used reasonable endeavours to identify alternative funding but has not been able to do so, and it would not be reasonable for the landlord to continue to provide accommodation or for the person who provided support to continue that provision in the circumstances.

- d The financial viability of the landlord or of supported accommodation or support services which the landlord provides, would, in the landlord's reasonable opinion, be threatened if the landlord were to continue to provide or fund a supported accommodation project of which the tenant's dwelling forms part and the landlord has used reasonable endeavours to identify alternative funding for the project but has not been able to do so. **Note** that a "supported accommodation project" is defined as supported accommodation comprising two or more dwellings in the same building or similar support services provided to tenants of multiple dwellings that are supported accommodation.
- e The tenant does not need the level of support services that are provided.
- f The tenant does not need any support services.
- g The dwelling has physical features intended to cater for specific needs to enable persons to live more independently than they could otherwise do so, and those physical features are not needed by the incumbent tenant.
- h The dwelling is physically unsuitable for the tenant's need for support services.

A Section 8 notice specifying this Ground 5F must provide the tenant with at least four weeks notice before the landlord can apply to the county court for a possession order. Reference to the possibility of possession being required on this ground must also be contained in the Statement of Terms given to the prospective tenant at the outset.

New mandatory Ground 5G – Tenancy granted for homelessness duty

This mandatory ground of possession 5G applies when to enable a Local Housing Authority to comply with duty to a homeless person under Section 193 Housing Act 1996, a third-party landlord grants a tenancy to the person owed the homeless duty. This ground for possession will then arise when the Local Housing Authority notifies the landlord that the tenancy is no longer required for the purposes of the Section 193 duty. Without this mandatory ground for possession, private landlords might be hesitant to work with local authorities in housing homeless people if they were unable to get the property back once the tenant had ceased to qualify for homeless accommodation.

Having received that notice from the local authority, the landlord may then serve notice seeking possession of the property provided that the expiry date of the Section 8 notice is no longer than 12 months from the original notification from the local authority. Note that Section 8ZA enables the county court to dispense with this particular requirement as regards timing where it is considered just and equitable to do so.

Note that this ground for possession does not apply where a local authority, in pursuance of its homeless duties, grants a tenancy directly, because local authority tenancies operate under a separate statutory regime as contained in the Housing Act 1985. A local authority tenancy can never be an assured tenancy under the Housing Act 1988. The ground for possession can only apply when a local authority arranges the letting through a third-party landlord. Section 193 of the 1996 Act refers to a council's duty to secure the availability of accommodation to a homeless person in priority need who has not become homeless intentionally.

A Section 8 notice specifying this Ground 5G must provide the tenant with at least four weeks notice before the landlord can apply to the county court for a possession order. Reference to the possibility of possession being required on this ground must also be contained in the Statement of Terms given to the prospective tenant at the outset.

New mandatory Ground 5H for possession of stepping stone accommodation

This ground for possession only applies to a landlord who is a registered provider of social housing or a charity and to a tenancy granted because the tenant met one or more eligibility conditions, as expressed in a written tenancy agreement. An 'eligibility condition' is defined to mean any of the following: that the tenant is in paid work or paid work of a specified description; or the tenant is actively seeking such paid work; the tenant is within a particular age range; the amount paid for that work; and the duration or expected duration of the work. The definition of paid work is also wide enough to include self-employment. This ground for possession will then arise if either the tenant no longer meets the specified eligibility conditions or the tenancy was granted temporarily to help the tenant transition to independent living and that temporary period has expired.

A Section 8 notice specifying this Ground 5H must provide the tenant with at least two months before the landlord can apply to the county court for a possession order. Reference to the possibility of possession being required on this ground must also be contained in the Statement of Terms given to the prospective tenant at the outset.

Amended mandatory Ground 6: redevelopment

This ground for possession has been substantially re-written by the 2025 Act and cross-refers to a table setting out the alternative circumstances to which this ground for possession arises and how it arises.

The intention of this ground of possession (as amended) is to enable a landlord to recover possession from an assured tenant in circumstances where there is a genuine intention, either by the immediate landlord or a superior landlord, to demolish or reconstruct the whole or a substantial part of the premises but the work cannot be carried out without the tenant giving up possession of the whole or part of the premises or providing access or other facilities to enable the work to be carried out. It follows that, where it is possible to do so, the tenant should first be given an opportunity to agree a variation to the tenancy to accommodate the proposed works. It is a further condition of obtaining possession under this ground that the assured tenancy began at least six months before possession is required, save where the landlord acquired its interest by compulsory purchase. This ground for possession also applies if the landlord seeking possession is a relevant social landlord and is also the party intending to carry out the work and that landlord previously gave the tenant a written statement of the landlord's wish to be able to recover possession on that ground. A registered social landlord seeking possession under this Ground 6 must also be in a position to show that suitable alternative accommodation will be made available for the displaced tenant.

A key change brought about by the 2025 Act is the abolition of the requirement that any landlord seeking to recover possession on this ground must have first acquired their interest in the premises before the grant of the relevant assured tenancy. A Section 8 notice claiming possession on this ground must give the tenants at least two months notice before possession proceedings can be launched.

Note also the obligation placed on registered social landlords relying on Ground G by Section 11 of the 1988 Act (as amended by Section 22 of the 2025 Act) to pay reasonable removal expenses to the displaced tenant. The same obligation to pay removable expenses also relates to Grounds 6A and 9 below.

Note also the new Section 8ZA of the 1988 Act which enables the court to dispense with the requirement that the works cannot be accommodated by a variation in the tenancy, where it is just and equitable to do so.

New mandatory Ground 6A – Possession of alternative accommodation provided during redevelopment

This new Ground 6A will apply to a social landlord seeking to repossess a dwelling house made available temporarily for the occupation by the tenant to enable redevelopment of another dwelling house which had been the tenant's only or principal home. The Section 8 notice period for this ground of possession is four months. **Note** also the obligation on the RSL to pay the displaced tenant's reasonable removal expenses as contained in the amended Section 11 of the 1998 Act (see above).

New mandatory ground for Possession 6B – To allow compliance with enforcement action

This new mandatory ground enables a landlord to recover possession of premises where necessary to comply with statutory housing enforcement action in any of the following circumstances:

a Letting the dwelling causes the landlord to breach a Banning Order under Section 16 Housing and Planning Act 2016 or would do so if the letting continued. [**Note** that a Banning order can be made by a first-tier tribunal on the application of a local housing authority where a landlord has previously been convicted of certain housing-related offences, including unlawful eviction or harassment. More information about banning orders is provided later in this book].

b An Improvement Notice under Section 11 or 12 of the Housing Act 2004

   i which specifies the dwelling or the premises within which the dwelling is contained, as requiring remedial action, and

   ii specifies overcrowding as the deficiency giving rise to the hazard in respect of which that remedial action is to be taken.

c Where a Prohibition Order is made under Section 20 or 21 Housing Act 2004 [following identification by the local housing authority of a Category 1 or Category 2 Hazard] and which prohibits use of: the dwelling house or shared utilities; for any purpose that is incompatible with continued occupation by the tenant.

d The dwelling house is in an HMO [house in multiple occupation] required to be licensed under Section 61 Housing Act 2004 and either: (i) the landlord applied for a licence which was refused, or (ii) the landlord held a licence which has been revoked.

e The dwelling house is required to be licensed under Section 85 Housing Act 2004 [Selective Part 3 Licensing] and either (i) the landlord has applied for licence under that Section 87, which was refused; or (ii) the landlord held a licence which has been revoked.

f The dwelling is an HMO which is licensed under Part 2 of the Housing Act 2004 or which is licensed under Part 3 of that Act and that HMO or house is occupied by more than the maximum number of households or persons specified in the license.

A Section 8 notice specifying this Ground 6B must provide the tenant with at least four months before the landlord can apply to the county court for a possession order.

Note that because of a new Section 11A to the 1998 Act (as inserted by Section 3(5 of the 2025 Act), a landlord who successfully obtains a possession order on this new Ground 6B may be required by the court to compensate the tenant for damage or loss sustained by the tenant as a result of the possession order. In deciding whether to order payment of compensation and if so the amounts of compensation, the court is required to take into account the circumstances which led to the Ground 6B becoming available to the landlord for obtaining possession, including any conduct by the tenant which caused or contributed to the availability of that Ground 6B. **Note** also that a compensation liability can arise even if the Ground 6B is combined with another ground for possession in the landlord's Section 8 notice.

Amended mandatory Ground 7 – Transmission of tenancy by will or intestacy

As simplified by the 2025 Act, this mandatory ground for possession applies if a tenancy has devolved under the will or intestacy of the former tenant and enables the landlord to begin possession proceedings no later than 12 months from the date of that death or, if the court so directs, the date the landlord became aware of that death. For the purpose of this mandatory ground, the landlord's subsequent acceptance of rent from the new tenant is not to be regarded in law as creating a new tenancy unless the landlord has also agreed in writing to any change in the tenancy. The Section 8 notice for this particular ground must give the tenant at least two months notice.

Mandatory Ground 7A – Conviction of a serious offence

This existing mandatory ground for possession is unchanged by the new legislation. As soon as a Section 8 notice has been served on the tenant under this Ground 7A, possession proceedings can be started immediately.

Mandatory Ground 7B – Disqualified by immigration status

This existing mandatory ground for possession is unchanged by the new legislation.

Mandatory Ground 8 – Rent arrears – as amended by the 2025 Act

As originally written, the court was obliged to order possession in circumstances when it was proved that the rent was at least eight weeks or two months in arrears both at the date the landlord's notice was served and also at the date of the possession hearing. The principal change brought about by the 2025 Act is that to qualify for possession under this ground, the landlord must now prove that the rent was at least 13 weeks or 3 months in arrears at the date the notice was served and again at the date of the hearing. A secondary change made by the 2025 Act is to discount from the arrears-calculation any award of universal credit which is due but has yet to be received by the tenant. A Section 8 notice specifying this mandatory ground must give the tenant at least four weeks notice before possession proceedings can be commenced.

Discretionary grounds of possession – Part II of Schedule 2 of the 1998 Act

The difference between the mandatory grounds of possession referred to above and which have been the subject of substantial amendment by the 2025 Act, and the nine discretionary grounds of possession listed in Part II of Schedule 2 of the 1998 Act (as 9 to 18) is that if a landlord is able to prove on a balance of probabilities one of the mandatory grounds of possession, a county court judge has no discretion to refuse an outright possession order. By contrast, Part II of Schedule 2 of the 1998 Act (as previously amended) contains a list of discretionary grounds of possession which a landlord can use to claim possession but which a judge is only obliged to grant when considered reasonable to do so. A possession order granted on one of the Part II discretionary grounds may also be suspended, which means that defaulting tenant will be given a last chance to make good the default before the possession order becomes absolute. A reason why a landlord may be tempted to use one of the Part II discretionary grounds to address tenants default is in terms of speed.

For example, discretionary Ground 10 enables a landlord to serve a Section 8 notice seeking possession almost as soon as the tenant begins to fall into rent arrears. That Section 8 notice then only has to give the defaulting tenant the minimum of four weeks notice before the landlord can commence possession proceedings.

Even if that possession order is eventually granted on suspended terms, a defaulting tenant who does not begin paying off their arrears will be evicted from the property. By contrast, a landlord who prefers to use mandatory Ground 8 to seek possession on the grounds of rent arrears, will have to allow those arrears to accumulate for three months before they can even begin serving their Section 8 notice and then wait a further four weeks before they can apply to the court for a possession order on that mandatory Ground 8.

Even where possession is sought on that mandatory ground, a defaulting tenant only has to reduce the arrears to less than three months on the date of the court hearing, to avoid eviction.

Whilst the 2025 Act has made substantive changes to the mandatory grounds for possession as outlined above, the Part II discretionary grounds of possession, as they existed immediately before 1 May 2026, have remained largely unchanged, save as regards the introduction of a new discretionary Ground 18 (see below), which will apply when a tenant in supported accommodation is not complying with the terms of their support.

What has changed for use of these discretionary grounds is a marginal extension of the lead-in notice periods before court proceedings can be started on any of those discretionary grounds. We have listed below a summary of those discretionary Grounds 9–17 as they currently exist together with details of updated lead-in periods.

Ground 9 – The availability of suitable alternative accommodation (two months). Note the additional obligation on an RSL placing reliance on this ground, to pay the tenant's reasonable removal expenses.
Ground 10 – There are some rent arrears (four weeks)
Ground 11 – Persistent delay in paying rent (four weeks)
Ground 12 – Breach of other tenancy obligations (two weeks)
Ground 13 – An occupant of the property has carried out acts of waste (two weeks)
Ground 14 – Antisocial behaviour on the part of an occupant or visitor to the property. Once a Section 8 notice has been served on this Ground 14, the landlord may commence possession proceedings immediately. **Note**: If a landlord is considering seeking possession of premises on this Ground 14, account must also be taken of Section 5 of the 2025 Act, which makes changes to Section 9A of the 1988 Act and sets out the statutory criteria to which the court must take account when considering whether to make a possession order. This discretionary Ground 14 relates to antisocial behaviour in circumstances where (in the absence of a conviction for a serious criminal offence), the landlord is unable to rely on the mandatory ground for possession contained in Ground 7A of the Schedule 1988 Act.

Where possession is claimed under the discretionary Ground 14, Section 9A of the 1988 Act requires the court to consider in particular the effect of the nuisance or annoyance on other people or the likely effect of that nuisance or annoyance if that behaviour is continued or repeated. The changes brought about by Section 5 of the 2025 Act now require the court, in addition, to consider whether the person against whom the possession order is being sought has co-operated with any attempt by the landlord to encourage the cessation of the antisocial behaviour. Specific provision is also now made as regards HMOs, which means that the court now must pay particular regard to the effect of the antisocial behaviour on other occupiers of the same premises who share accommodation or facilities.

Ground 14ZA An occupant of the property has been convicted of an indictable offence committed at the scene of a riot in the UK. (two weeks).
Ground 14A – Which enables a registered social landlord to evict a domestic abuser (two weeks).
Ground 15 – Damage to furnishings (two weeks).

Ground 16 – Cessation of tenant's employment (service tenancy) – (two months).

Ground 17 – Tenancy obtained on the basis of false representations (two weeks).

Ground 18 – Supported Accommodation (four weeks) – This new discretionary ground for possession will apply when the dwelling house is supported accommodation and the tenant has unreasonably refused to engage with the support services provided as part of that accommodation or alternatively acted in a way that is fundamentally inconsistent with the provision of support services to the tenant or another person being in the supported accommodation.

Note that where a Section 8 notice is issued on multiple possession grounds (with different lead in periods), the length notice given to the tenant must be calculated on the longest of those grounds.

4 The process of recovering possession

In the previous chapter, we looked at the statutory grounds of possession which a landlord has to prove to recover possession of premises from an assured tenant under the new law. In this chapter, we look at the process of recovering possession of those premises.

Notices to quit

We start with notices to quit, the traditional way in which any unprotected periodic tenancy can be terminated either by the landlord or the tenant. Although a landlord cannot unilaterally require an assured tenant to vacate except by proving one of the statutory grounds listed in the previous chapter, there's nothing to prevent a residential tenant terminating their tenancy in that way. Once given, a tenant's notice to quit cannot be withdrawn unilaterally and on its expiry, the tenant no longer has any contractual right to remain in the premises but cannot be forcibly evicted without a court order and through due process.

The abolition of fixed-term residential tenancies by the 2025 Act means that a residential tenant can now terminate their assured tenancy at any time on as little two months prior written notice expiring on a rent day, even if their original tenancy was granted for a longer fixed term. In some cases, the landlord may have also agreed to a shorter period of notice.

In its original form, Section 5 of the Protection from Eviction Act 1977 required any notice to quit, whether given by a landlord or a tenant, to be in the prescribed format and giving not less than four weeks to the other party before the notice could take effect. The position has now changed for assured tenancies by a new Section 1ZA to the 1988 Act (as introduced by Section 19 of the 2025 Act. This now requires a notice to quit given by a tenant to their landlord, to be given in writing at least two months before the date it is stated to take effect, unless the landlord has previously agreed in writing to accept shorter notice.

For other residential tenancies, excluded by Schedule 1 of the 1988 Act from being assured tenancies, the minimum notice under the 1977 Act remains at four weeks. The previous Section 5 reference to a landlord's notice to quit

DOI: 10.1201/9781003681403-4

has been deleted in its entirety. **Note** also the new Section 5A to the 1988 Act (as introduced by Section 20 of the 2025 Act), which voids any contractual stipulation requiring a tenant's notice to quit to be given in any particular form. It would also seem that going forward, it may be possible for a tenant's notice to be given electronically. This is because Section 5A2 defines '*means of giving notice in writing*' as being sufficient if the words of the notice are represented or reproduced in a visible form. Once given, a tenant's notice to quit may only be withdrawn with the landlord's written agreement.

It has *never* been possible for a landlord to terminate a residential assured tenancy by a simple notice to quit, not under the 1988 Act as originally written nor as amended by the 2025 Act. The correct statutory processes have to be followed (see below). However, we see no reason why a residential tenancy which is neither assured nor protected under other tenancy legislation cannot be terminated by a landlord's notice to quit.

Obtaining possession of residential premises after 1 May 2026

After 1 May 2026, when the new law took effect, the only way in which a landlord can unilaterally terminate a residential assured tenancy is by service of a compliant notice under Section 8 of the 1988 Act (as amended).

Where notice had previously been served by the landlord seeking eviction under the now abolished Section 21, transitional provisions preserve the validity of that Section 21 notice, so long as possession proceedings in the county court are issued before the end of July 2026. If legal proceedings have not already been lodged with the court before 1 August 2026, notices served before 1 May 2026 will automatically lapse.

Those transitional protections cannot apply to any assured shorthold tenancy entered into after 1 January 2026, as even under the original 1988 Act legislation, a Section 21 notice could not have been served within the first six months of a tenancy. The same 31 July 2026 cut-off date also applies to any landlord notice previously served under Section 8 of the 1988 Act, or one of the possession grounds applicable before the changes took effect on 1 May 2026.

The only exception to the 31 July 2026 cut off for the initiation of county court proceedings on any landlord's notice issued before 1 May 2026 is if any Section 8 ground for possession related to rent arrears and the landlord was prevented from issuing legal proceedings because the tenant was in a 'breathing space" under The Debt Respite Scheme (Breathing Space Moratorium and Mental Health Crisis Moratorium) (England and Wales) Regulations 2020.

Where the tenant is in 'breathing space', a landlord will have eight weeks from the date that the breathing space ends to start court proceedings. A 'standard breathing space' protects a debtor from creditor action for up to 60 days. A mental health breathing space is only available to someone receiving mental health crisis treatment and who requires stronger protection. A mental health-related breathing space will last as long as the person's mental health crisis treatment exists plus an additional 30 days. The fact that a tenant is in 'breathing space' does not prevent a landlord from issuing possession proceedings for reasons not related to rent arrears.

Where a landlord's Section 8 or Section 21 notice of seeking possession has lapsed because legal proceedings have not been issued before the 1 August 2026 cut off, the landlord will have lost the right to evict under the abolished Section 21 and (assuming that the necessary grounds exist) will need to restart the process and issue a new Section 8 notice using one of the new statutory grounds for possession. Likewise, a lapsed Section 8 notice issued under the old grounds of possession will have to be restarted with a fresh Section 8 notice and placing reliance on one of the new or amended grounds for possession. We now look at the process of issuing a landlord's notice seeking possession after the new provisions came into force on 1 May 2026.

Legal barriers to a Section 8 eviction

The first step for any landlord wishing to serve a Section 8 notice of possession is to address the legal barriers which might otherwise invalidate the Section 8 notice and a judge's ability to grant a possession order, even if the statutory ground is proved.

Even before 1st May 2026, it was impossible for a landlord to issue a notice seeking possession under Section 21 of the 1988 Act if there were irregularities regarding the holding of any tenant deposit. There are also additional legal barriers for any landlord seeking possession of premises on the basis of a Section 21 notice issued before 1 May 2026. The landlord will *not* be able to rely on the validity of a preserved Section 21 notice issued before 1 May 2026 if:

- The landlord had previously received an improvement notice or notice of emergency remedial action from the local housing authority, and the landlord has not complied with the requirements of that notice.
- The landlord has not refunded any unlawful charges or prohibited payments (see later).
- The landlord has not provided a valid gas safety certificate (where applicable), an energy performance certificate and the correct version of the 'How to Rent Guide', when the tenancy was first entered into.

Following the post-1 May 2026 abolition of Section 21 evictions, a new precondition for service of a Section 8 notice using one of the new or amended statutory grounds is that the landlord will be required to demonstrate that any tenant deposit was protected in a government approved scheme and landlord had complied with the requirements of that scheme when the deposit was received and that the landlord gave the tenant the required information about the deposit protection scheme. Such deposit information to be given by the landlord to the tenant must include details of the relevant deposit protection scheme, confirmation of the amount protected, landlord contact details and information on how the tenant can get their deposit back at the end of a tenancy.

The only exception to this deposit protection precondition is if the landlord uses Grounds 7A or 14, which relate to antisocial behaviour. It is also illegal for a landlord to take a deposit in any form other than money and the landlord must have returned any items taken from the tenant before possession can be obtained on any of the statutory grounds.

Note that once the new landlord database (see Chapter 10) becomes operational (expected 2027/8), it will also be a requirement for Section 8 possession proceedings that the landlord as well as the dwelling are appropriately registered on the new private rented sector database.

Having cleared any statutory preconditions to the issue of the notice seeking possession, it is just as important that any notice served is in the correct statutory format. Any Section 8 notice seeking possession served on a tenant before 1 May 2026 would have had to be in statutory Form 3. Any statutory notice seeking possession served after 1 May 2026 and relying on one of the new or amended statutory grounds of possession will have to be in the new Form 3A. The only exception is for registered social landlords who will, for the time being, continue to use the old Form 3.

Government guidance updated on 19 December 2025, titled 'Repossessing Your Privately Rented Property on or after 1st May 2026', provides guidance on the filling out of the new Form 3A. It stresses that new statutory Grounds 1 and 1A (landlord moving in or selling) cannot be used until 12 months after the tenancy started, even though the notice itself can be served earlier. There are also other statutory grounds for possession in which a landlord is prevented from using in a Section 8 notice unless the tenant had been informed in writing at the start of the tenancy that such grounds for possession might be used. These special grounds of possession for which prior warning is required include (summarised):

- Where the landlord's own proprietary interest in the property is held under a superior lease which is ending (Grounds 2ZA and 2ZB).
- Ground 4A for evicting students where the property is required for new students in line with an academic year.
- Ground 5C for ending a tenancy which was connected with the tenant's job, where the tenant's job has ended or the purposes for which the accommodation was provided has ended and the landlord intends to provide the accommodation to another worker.

As will be seen later in this book, it is now illegal for landlords to quote in their Section 8 notices grounds for possession which they do not believe to be true.

If a tenant does not leave the property on the expiration of the Section 8 notice, the landlord's next step is to apply to the county court for a possession order.

In the case of notices served before 1 May 2026, the cut-off date for the initiation of those court proceedings is 31 July 2026. For Section 8 notices served after 1 May 2026, landlords have from the date the minimum notice period expires until 12 months from the issue of the notice to issue possession proceedings; after which the notice lapses and the landlord will have to restart the process with a new Section 8 notice.

What this means is that for a notice issued on one of the new non-fault grounds, landlords only have an interval of 8 months from the four-month expiry of the notice to issue court proceedings. Another consequence from the abolition of the old Section 21 evictions, which were entirely process driven, is that landlords relying on one of the new Section 8 grounds will not be able to use the accelerated possession procedure. In its place, the government intends to introduce a new digital possession service, to be known as The Possession Claim Online Service (PCOL), only for possession claims based on rent arrears. For all other possession claims, landlords will be required to issue proceedings on paper.

Landlords using the new PCOL will need to give proof of payments due and received for up to a maximum of two years. The government has also issued a new version of Claim Form N5 for paper-based applications to the court. The court fee for an application for possession is currently set at £404. On receipt of a completed application with the correct supporting information, the court will set a hearing date, and there will be an opportunity for the tenant to file a defence within 14 days of receiving papers. Depending on which ground for possession is used, the required evidence might include:

- A statement of rent owed by the tenant
- Evidence of antisocial behaviour, like witness statements or documents showing a serious offence or breach of a court order
- Photographs showing damage to the property
- Evidence that the landlord intends to sell the property, which could include proof that an estate agent has been instructed
- Evidence that the tenant has breached other terms of the tenancy agreement, such as an unlawful subletting

Save where the tenant voluntarily vacates following receipt of a Section 8 notice, all possession applications will now proceed to a hearing before a judge, with any of the following possible outcomes:

- The hearing may be adjourned to a later date if the judge is not able to deal fully with the matter on the day.
- The possession claim may be dismissed if the landlord is unable to prove the ground of possession relied upon in the Section 8 notice or if there is some other material procedural irregularity on the landlord's part.
- The judge will make an outright possession order if the landlord is able to prove one of the mandatory grounds for possession listed in the Section 8 notice and provided that there is no material irregularity in the process which the landlord has adopted to bring the case to court. It is also possible that a judge may make an outright possession order if one of the Part II discretionary possession grounds is proved and the judge considers that an outright possession order is reasonable in the circumstances.
- The judge may make a suspended possession order, which will give the tenant a last chance to pay off any rent arrears or make good any other default which is capable of remedy. If the tenant complies with the terms of the suspended order and pays off any associated court costs, the threat of eviction will fall away. A suspended order can only be made when a landlord relies on one of the Part II discretionary grounds for possession and the judge does not consider it necessary to make an outright possession order. If the tenant subsequently breaks the terms of the suspended order, the landlord can apply for the issue of a bailiff's warrant using Form 325A.

An outright possession order will usually require the tenant to vacate the premises within 14 days. However, when making an outright possession order, a judge may allow a tenant up to six weeks to vacate if the tenant would otherwise suffer extreme hardship if forced to leave earlier. A judge can also delay eviction for longer when possession is ordered on one of the discretionary grounds.

When granting a possession order, a judge may add a money judgement covering any existing rent arrears plus the costs of the proceedings. It is also important to note that getting a possession order from a county court judge may not be the end of the eviction process. Once a possession order has been obtained (or a suspended possession order has been activated), a landlord may be faced with any of the following outcomes:

i The tenant may voluntarily vacate on or before the date the possession order is expressed to take effect. In those circumstances, all that the landlord or the landlord's agent has to do is to re-secure the premises against entry.

ii The tenant does not comply with the possession order requiring them to vacate. In those circumstances, all that a landlord can do is to apply to the court for a warrant of possession using Form N325 for an outright possession order or Form N325A to activate a suspended possession order. At current rates, it costs £148 to apply for that warrant of possession.

iii The tenant may have appealed the possession order. Note that a landlord also has 21 days to appeal the refusal of a possession order, provided that at the end of the initial hearing the landlord's representative has asked the judge to give reasons for their decision and for permission to appeal.

iv A tenant can apply to have the possession order set aside if they were not able to attend the hearing and can provide sufficient reason for their absence. Where a possession order is set aside, the claim will remain open and the tenant will still have an opportunity to present a defence.

v Even where a date has been set for an eviction, the tenant can still apply to the court to suspend the warrant but only if the landlord relied on one of the discretionary possession grounds or if the landlord has agreed to let the tenant stay for longer.

Note that whilst an assured periodic tenant cannot be forcibly evicted without a court order, there is nothing in law preventing a residential tenant from voluntarily relinquishing possession before a court order is obtained. Particularly if they believe that a possession order would otherwise be inevitable and want to avoid the stress, inconvenience and costs of a court case. This is why the 2025 Act has introduced robust provisions to ensure that a landlord does not do anything calculated to mislead their tenant into thinking that their right to possession is stronger than it actually is. These are fully explained in a later chapter.

The 2025 Act also adds to the general remedies available to tenants under statute or common law, with new regulatory protections to ensure that residential landlords act responsibly and within the law. These comprise a range of financial penalties as well as the possibility of prosecution and complaint to the newly created Housing Ombudsman, which are fully explained in a later chapter. In the next chapter, we explain each of these new landlord duties. Again, these will be fully explained.

5 Advance rent, deposits and rent variation

Existing statutory provisions relating to the protection of tenants deposits as introduced by Part 5 Chapter 4 of the Housing Act 2004 remain in force. Failure to comply with these statutory deposit protection requirements previously inhibited a landlord's right to recover possession under the old Section 21 of the Housing Act 1988 (since abolished by the 2025 Act). What has since changed is the new Section 215 of the Housing Act 1988 (as substituted by Section 26(5) of the 2025 Act), which now prevents the County Court from making an order *on any Ground* (except for the antisocial behaviour grounds 7A or 14) for possession of a dwelling let on an assured tenancy if any associated tenant deposit is not being held in accordance with an authorised scheme or alternatively has not been returned to the tenant or if there are other irregularities relating to the holding of that deposit.

The Tenant Fees Act 2019 (which prohibits certain charges being made by a landlord to its tenant) remains in force with only consequential amendments. The new position as regards tenant deposits as well as any requirements for advance rent are set out below.

Section 8 of the 2025 Act (prohibition of rent in advance after lease entered into except initial rent)

For 'lease', read 'tenancy agreement'. Section 8 of the 2025 Act (which adds a new Section 4B in the Tenant Fees Act 2019), prevents a landlord or a landlord's agent from demanding or accepting advance rent from a prospective tenant until the tenancy agreement has actually been signed. However, it is also recognized within Section 8 that there may be a short interval between the date a tenancy agreement is signed and the actual start date of the tenancy. That interval is referred to in the new Section 4B(12) as the 'permitted pre-tenancy period'. There is nothing in the new legislation to prevent a landlord requiring the first month's rent to be paid in that interval between the date the tenancy agreement is signed and the date the tenant's right to occupy the premises actually starts.

DOI: 10.1201/9781003681403-5

Once the tenancy has actually started, future rental payments will fall due on the dates agreed in the tenancy agreement and a landlord will not be able to require a tenant to make any rent payment before that date. The terms of any tenancy agreement which state otherwise are rendered void by the new Section 4B(1). However, there is nothing in the Tenant Fees Act 2019 to prevent landlords recharging for lost keys or for receiving notification of any transmission of the tenancy. In each case, the landlord can only charge up to a capped amount.

Asking for a rental payment before a tenancy agreement has been signed renders a landlord or letting agent liable to a civil penalty of up to £5,000 on a first breach. Repeat breaches can result in prosecution or a monetary penalty of up to £30,000.

The rule against acceptance of advance rent does not apply to registered social landlords. Nor does it apply in circumstances where a local authority agrees with a private landlord to pay rent in advance to facilitate a letting to someone who qualifies as homeless. This is not a breach as a local authority is not a 'relevant person' in the Tenant Fees Act 2019 and therefore exempt from the rules relating to advance rent. In those circumstances there would also be nothing to prevent a private landlord seeking an agreed regular sum every six months from the local authority if the tenancy was set up to meet the local authority's homelessness duty.

Rental deposits

The position regarding rental deposits is different from advance rent and is also governed by the Tenant Fees Act 2019 as amended by the 2025 Act. The 2019 Act allows landlords or their letting agent to ask a prospective tenant to pay a holding deposit to reserve a property, which cannot be more than a week's rent.

If the tenancy goes ahead, that holding deposit may then be applied in part payment to the first month's rent. However, a letting agent cannot hold more than one holding deposit in relation to any property, which must first be returned to the paying party if a holding deposit is to be accepted from another prospective tenant.

Under the 2019 Act, the maximum tenancy deposit which a landlord can seek is five weeks rent if the annual rent for that property is less than £50,000. If the annual rental is above £50,000, a landlord can ask for a deposit of up to six weeks rent

Rent variation and other tenancy terms

A significant change brought about by the 2025 Act is that the threat of eviction can no longer be used as a means of increasing the rent payable under an assured tenancy.

However, Sections 13 and 14 of the Housing Act 1988 have always provided statutory machinery enabling a residential landlord to increase the rent payable under an assured tenancy.

Going forward, this statutory machinery, as amended by the 2025 Act, provides the only means by which a landlord can impose a rental increase on their assured tenant.

As originally drawn, these statutory provisions required the landlord to serve a statutory notice of the increased rent on the tenant. That new rent would then take effect on the date specified in the notice unless, within the limited time available to do so, the tenant had made an application to the First-tier Tribunal (Property Chamber) (Residential Property).

In other words it was, 'time of the essence'. Tenants, who did not exercise their statutory right to refer the increase to the tribunal, would lose the right to do so once the notice had taken effect. The statutory process for increasing rents was also dis-applied, in circumstances where the tenancy agreement contained its own contractual provisions for upward review of the monthly rent. But whatever the statutory machinery might say, the reality for any assured shorthold tenant was that they had no choice but to pay whatever increased rent the landlord demanded, to avoid the possibility of a Section 21 eviction.

With the abolition of the old Section 21 no-fault eviction, assured tenants now have a choice whether to accept or challenge a proposed rent increase. The new position regarding rental variation as introduced by the 2025 Act is now summarised below:

1 Any contractual rent review mechanism contained in a tenancy agreement which would have otherwise displaced the statutory rent review mechanism, no longer has legal effect.
2 There's a separate statutory rent review machinery for registered providers of social housing (other than local authorities), which are now referred to in this legislation as being 'low-cost tenancies'.
3 The minimum period for a landlord's Notice of Increase (for a private market rent letting) is now extended to two months.
4 It is still possible for a landlord and a tenant to reach written agreement on a varied rent.
5 For a 'low-cost tenancy' (see above), the minimum period of notice of increased rent is reduced to one month instead of two months for other private lettings.
6 A new Section 13(B) to the Housing Act 1988 allows the tribunal to determine whether a notice of rent increase is valid.
7 In an echo of the old Rent Acts, Section 7(3) of the 2025 Act introduces new Subsections 14(A1); (A2); and (A3), to Section 14 of the 1988 Act. which gives a general right to an assured tenant (not occupying under a 'low-cost tenancy'), to apply to the tribunal for a *rent reduction* save where the rent payable has been subject to a previous tribunal determination or if

more than six months have elapsed since the beginning of the tenancy. In other words, a new tenant has six months to apply to a tribunal to challenge the rent previously negotiated at the start of the tenancy. This is an addition to the right a tenant has to challenge a notice of increase by application to the tribunal. However, this right for a tenant to apply for a rent reduction does not apply to low-cost tenancies. What this means is that almost as soon as a new tenancy agreement has been signed, a new tenant can apply to a first-tier tribunal for a rent reduction. The landlord will then have a choice either to agree to a lower rent with the incoming tenant or go to the cost and inconvenience of defending the negotiated rent before a tribunal. Once that tribunal decision has been made, the tenant cannot have a second bite at the cherry. And if no application is made to the tribunal within the first six months by the new tenant, that risk will fall away. Surprisingly, the fact that a tribunal may have made a recent decision relating to a previous tenancy of the same premises does not bar the incoming tenant from making a new application within the first six months of their tenancy.

8 A new Section 14ZA states that where (on a tenant's application for a reduced rent) the tribunal has made a determination as to the applicable rent, the new rent will be the lower of the open market rent or the existing tenancy rent the subject of challenge.

9 Where the tribunal has made its determination as a result of a landlord's notice of increase, a new increased rent cannot be backdated and will not take effect earlier than date of the tribunal's decision and may (to avoid hardship) be expressed to take effect at a later date.

6 Marketing and documenting a tenancy

In the last chapter, we looked at new 2025 Act restrictions on the holding of advance rent and tenancy deposits. We now look at other express duties which the 2025 Act imposes on landlords of assured periodic tenancies from 1st May 2026.

Summary of new duties on a landlord or letting agent when marketing premises for letting on an assured periodic tenancy

1 Any landlord or landlord agent advertising residential premises for letting must include in any written advertisement the actual amount of the rent which will be paid by the incoming tenant. Section 56 of the 2025 Act, which imposes this new landlord obligation, also prohibits landlords from inviting or encouraging anyone to offer rent exceeding that stated in the advertisement. The only exception to this rule is the traditional 'To Let' sign actually displayed on the dwelling or at the building within which the dwelling is situated. Nor does this restriction apply to offers which are made verbally. Section 57 of the 2025 Act makes clear that a landlord or letting agent who breaches this obligation can receive a financial penalty of up to £7,000. **Note** that we can see nothing in Section 56 which prevents a landlord accepting a negotiated rent *below* the advertised amount. However we would caution against any temptation on the part of landlords or landlord's agent to deliberately overprice a prospective letting as this may enable an incoming tenant to successfully challenge the overpriced rent under Section 14 (A1) (A2) and (A3) of the 1988 Act (as substituted) and otherwise deter good prospective tenants from expressing their interest in renting the property.

2 Not to discriminate (either directly or indirectly) against prospective tenants who have children or who are in receipt of state benefits of any description (see below).

3 Not to accept rent before the tenancy agreement is actually signed (save one week's holding deposit).

DOI: 10.1201/9781003681403-6

4. Not to offer or enter into a fixed-term residential assured tenancy. Contravention of this statutory requirement might be as simple as adding an end date to the tenancy agreement.
5. With the exception of the first month's rent taken on the signing of the tenancy agreement, not to take any other advance rent, which will only become due on the payment dates specified in the tenancy agreement.
6. Not to accept a tenancy deposit of more than five weeks rent (if the annual rent is less than £50,000) or six weeks if the annual rent is more than £50,000.
7. To provide required tenant deposit protection information.
8. To provide the updated 'How to Rent' guide.
9. Mandatory safety and compliance information: including gas safety certificate (where there is a gas supply); energy performance certificate; and electrical installation condition report.
10. To provide the incoming tenant with a Statement of Tenancy Terms, which can either be contained within the tenancy agreement itself or as a separate document (see below).
11. Once new landlord registration requirements come into force, landlords will also have to provide the incoming tenant with the landlord's registration number.

Note that for residential assured tenancies already in existence on 1 May 2026, landlords are required to provide to each of those existing tenants, and within one month (expiring 31st May 2026), a Tenant Information Sheet, in the prescribed form and explaining the statutory changes to the landlord and the tenant relationship which took place on 1st May 2026.

Duty to provide a Statement of Tenancy Terms

The importance of a Statement of Tenancy Terms is that both the landlord and the tenant know exactly what the terms of an assured periodic tenancy are and also to provide a benchmark against which the performance of their respective contractual rights and obligations can be measured. A well-drawn statement of tenancy terms will also alert an incoming tenant to any specific non-fault possession grounds which the landlord may wish to rely on to bring the tenancy to an end in the future

Historically, it has always been possible to create a periodic tenancy simply by granting someone exclusive possession of premises in return for a rent. In the absence of a written lease or tenancy agreement, a periodic tenancy will then be presumed in law and attract the legal protections which would apply to any written residential or commercial tenancy.

Whilst it may still be legally possible to create a residential tenancy in this way, the position has now changed for new assured periodic tenancies by the insertion of a new Section 16D to the 1988 Act (as introduced by Section 12 of the 2025 Act). These new provisions require a residential landlord to provide an assured periodic tenant with a Statement of Terms. This statement may either be contained within a conventional tenancy agreement or provided as a written record of the agreed terms.

That Statement of Terms must be provided before the commencement of the assured tenancy and contain such information as may be specified by regulations. This will include prescribed information about the tenancy, the accommodation let under the tenancy, details of the named landlord and the tenant and the respective rights of the landlord and tenant. The Statement of Terms should also specify any of the following mandatory grounds on which the landlord may seek possession, namely:

- Ground 1B – Sale of dwelling under rent-to-buy
- Ground 2ZA – Possession when superior lease ends
- Ground 2ZB – Possession when superior lease ends
- Ground 2ZC – Possession by superior landlord
- Ground 2ZD – Possession by superior landlord
- Grounds 5 to 5H – Special grounds relating to ministers of religion, agricultural workers, employment requirements, supported accommodation, homeless accommodation, steppingstone accommodation
- Ground 18 – Supported accommodation

Note that although the right for a landlord to specify these particular grounds of possession in the tenancy agreement or other statement of terms is expressed by the new Section 16D(3) in permissive terms, a landlord who fails to specify any of these possible grounds for recovering possession may later inhibit their ability to rely on any of those specified mandatory grounds for possession, should the need arise. For this reason, when entering into a new residential tenancy, it is important that landlords take extra care when drafting the Statement of Terms to ensure that it covers every non-fault ground of possession on which the landlord may later wish to rely to recover possession of those premises. There may be no second chance.

Information sheets for residential tenancies already in existence on 1 May 2026

For an assured tenancies already in existence on 1 May 2026 (including those former fixed-term tenancies converted by operation of law into assured periodic tenancies), Paragraph 7(2) of Schedule 6 to the 2025 Act requires the landlord to give to their tenant specified information in writing about the changes made by the 2025 Act and which is required to be given by regulations made by the Secretary of State and which must be issued by close of business on 31 May 2026.

The Assured (Private Rented Sector) (Written Statement of Terms and Information Sheet) (England) Regulations 2026 now describe in detail the core information which a landlord must include in a legally compliant Statement of Terms for new tenancies as well as these Statutory Information Sheet to be given by the end of May 2026 for existing tenants. The purpose of the latter is to tell existing assured tenants (including former assured shorthold tenants what they need to know regarding the change in their tenancy status), their lifetime security of tenure and the new rights which are available to those existing tenants.

Regulation 2 (required content of written Statement of Terms, etc.) applies to all assured tenancies entered into from 1 May 2026 (with the exception of social housing assured tenancies). That detail is now set out at length in the schedule to those regulations, and it can be summarised as follows, using the same paragraph numbering:

1 The name of the landlord (or landlords where more than person comprise the landlord).
2 The name of the tenant or tenants.
3 An address in England or Wales at which notices (including legal notifications) can be served on the landlord by the tenant.
4 The address of the property let on the tenancy.
5 The date on which the tenant is first entitled to possession under the tenancy. [**Note** that this cannot be assumed to be the date the tenancy agreement is physically signed unless that is the date specified for the tenant to take up occupation].
6 The rent payable under the tenancy and when it is due.
7 A statement explaining that if the landlord proposes to increase the rent under the tenancy, the landlord must first serve notice in accordance with Section 13 of the 1988 Act [see above].
8 Where under the terms of the tenancy, a relevant bill payment is payable from the tenant to the landlord, that must be stated within the tenancy agreement as well as stating whether it is paid as part of the rent or in addition to the rent. In circumstances where bills are expressed to be payable in addition to the rent, the tenancy terms must explain how that additional amount will be calculated and also how and when the tenant will be notified of the amount of each payment and when it is due. **Note** that a 'relevant bill payment' is defined by the regulations to be the payment: in respect of council tax; for or in connection with the provision of a utility (meaning gas, electricity or other fuel; water or sewerage); towards energy efficiency improvements under a green deal plan; the television licence or the provision of a communication service (meaning telephone, internet, cable or satellite television).
9 If the requirements of Section 213 Housing Act 2004 (deposit protection schemes) apply to the tenancy and if so, the amount of the tenancy deposit.

10 If Section 5(1) of the Protection From Eviction Act 1977 (notices to quit by tenants under assured tenancies) applies in relation to the tenancy including the minimum written notice a tenant must provide to their landlord when giving notice to quit the property. **Note** that although the maximum notice an outgoing tenant must provide is limited to two months expiring on a rent payment date, there may be circumstances where the landlord is willing to commit to a shorter notice period.

11 If Section 5 of the 1988 Act (security of tenure) applies to the tenancy, the Statement of Terms must include an explanation that in most circumstances a landlord can only end the tenancy by obtaining a court possession order followed by the execution of that order. Also, that a landlord seeking to obtain a possession order must usually serve on the tenant a notice of proceedings in the prescribed format and specifying the ground of possession relied on, together with the minimum period of notice required for that particular ground of possession.

12 If Section 9A of the Housing Act 1985 (fitness for human habitation of dwellings in England) applies to the tenancy, the statement explains that the landlord is obliged to ensure that the property is legally fit for human habitation.

13 A statement that (to the extent required under Section 11 of the Housing Act 1985), the landlord is legally obliged to keep in repair the structure and exterior of the property (including drains, gutters and external pipes). This will include keeping in repair and proper working order the installations in the property for the supply of water, gas and electricity and for sanitation (including basins, sinks and other sanitary conveniences), but not other fixtures, fittings and appliances for making use of the supply of water, gas or electricity, The obligation also extends to keeping in repair and in proper working order the installations in the property for heating and hot water. **Note** that there is a statutory exception to these landlord obligations if the property is contained in premises for which the right to manage has been acquired by an RTM company under chapter 1 of Part 2 of the Commonhold and Leasehold Reform Act 2002, where such management arrangement still subsists.

14 If Regulation 3 of the Electrical Safety Standards in the Private Rented Sector and Social Rented Sector (England) Regulations 2020 applies to the property, a statement explaining that the landlord is legally obliged to do the following:

a To ensure that relevant electricity safety standards are met during the occupation of the property.

b To ensure that relevant electrical installations are inspected and tested by a qualified person at least every five years, or sooner if required by the electrical report (see below).

c To obtain a written report from the person who conducted the inspection and test and which gives the results of that inspection and test and the date by which the next inspection and test is required and to supply a copy of that report to the tenant.

15 Where there is a gas supply, a statement explaining that the landlord is obliged by regulation 36 of the Gas Safety Installation and Use Regulations 1998:

a To ensure the relevant gas fittings and associated flues are maintained in a safe condition.
b To ensure that every relevant appliance and flue is checked for safety by someone approved by the Health and Safety Executive and at intervals to be determined in accordance with the 1998 Regulations.
c To ensure that a written record in respect of every appliance or flue which has been checked is made and that a copy of the record is given to the tenant.

16 Where applicable, information about Section 190 of the Equality Act 2010 (improvements to let dwelling houses), including in particular: that Section 90 prevents a landlord from unreasonably withholding consent to a tenant's application to make an improvement (within the meaning of Section 190) in circumstances where a disabled person occupies or intends to occupy the premises as their only or main home and that the improvement is likely to facilitate the disabled person's enjoyment of the premises having regard to their disability, save as regards any like provision already within the tenancy. **Note** that this provision does not apply to a protected or statutory tenancy and only to the extent that the tenant is entitled (with the consent of the landlord) to make those improvements within the meaning of Section 190(9) of the 2010 Act,
17 A statement explaining that the tenant may ask their landlord for permission to keep a pet at the property in accordance with Section 16A of the 1988 Act, provided that the landlord consents, with the proviso that such landlord consent cannot be unreasonably refused.
18 If the tenancy is a tenancy of supported accommodation (within the meaning of Paragraph 12(10) of Schedule 2 to the 1988 Act) a statement to that effect and an explanation of why it is granted as such a tenancy

These Regulations also provide a link to a PDF containing the Information Sheet which must be provided to existing tenants who were already in occupation before 1st May 2026. This PDF must be downloaded exactly as written and the emailed or delivered hard-copy to each of those tenants. The Information Sheet explains the automatic conversion of the former fixed-term assured shorthold into the new assured period tenancy; the abolition of Section 21 evictions; the statutory process for rent increases; how the tenant can end the tenancy; keeping a pet; student lettings; and where those tenants can go for further advice.

As well as the new duty on a residential landlord to provide a Statement of Terms, as well as an Information Sheet to existing tenant,s a new Section 16E(1) (as inserted by Section 13 of the 2025 Act), imposes the following additional continuing duties on a residential landlord (or anyone representing a residential landlord other than someone carrying out a regulated legal activity) which are all expressed in negative terms:

Continuing landlord duties

Following on from the landlord duties which apply when residential landlord enters into a new assured tenancy, the following continuing landlord duties also apply as listed below

a Not to purport to bring the tenancy to an end by service of a notice to quit [as distinguished from notice served in accordance with the legal requirements of the 1988 Act as amended and any associated regulations]. The *Enforcement Guidance* (referred to in a later chapter), describes a notice to quit as a written document (perhaps even a text or Whatsapp message) describing itself as a notice to quit ending the tenancy and requiring the tenant to vacate the property by a certain date,

b Not to purport to bring the tenancy to an end, or require that it is brought to an end, orally;

c Not to serve on the Tenant a purported notice of possession [as distinguished from a formal possession order issued by the court]. A '*purported notice of possession*' is defined by Section 16M of the 1988 Act as being any written document which is not in accordance with Section 8 of the 1988 Act but pretends to be such a notice or alternatively pretends to end an assured tenancy on one of the Schedule 2 grounds but is neither a claim form nor document produced in relation to court proceedings for possession of the dwelling.

d Not to rely on any possession ground contained in schedule 2 of the 1988 Act as amended by the 2025 Act, where the person serving the notice does not reasonably believe that the landlord will or may be able to obtain an order for possession on that ground.

e Not to rely on any of the possession grounds contained in Grounds 1B; 2ZA to 2ZD; 4.5 to 5H or 18 [see above] if no reference to those grounds was made in the Statement of Terms. **Note** also Section 16M(2) of the 1988 Act, which states that a person 'relies' on a Schedule 2 ground where a person [who may not be the actual landlord but someone claiming to represent that landlord] serves the tenant with a notice under Section 8 (whether genuine or pretend) asserting that the landlord is able to obtain an order for possession on the stated Schedule 2 ground or, having not served any such notice, issues a court claim for possession.

f To prevent abuse, where possession is gained on mandatory grounds 1 or 1A (landlord requires property for own occupation or re-sale – see above), a new Section 16E(2) of the 1988 Act, there is a prohibition on the landlord re-letting the same premises during the 'restricted period' [see above]. New Section 16E(3) extends this prohibition to marketing the premises for re-letting, either by the landlord or anyone engaged by the landlord as part of a 'letting business'.

7 The cost of getting it wrong

The duty to enforce

The primary enforcing authority for the purposes of the Renters' Rights Act 2025 is the local housing authority. These are the district or unitary councils having statutory housing functions, which includes the London boroughs as well as the Common Council for the City of London. The definition excludes those county councils in two-tier administrative areas, where public functions are split between the District Council, which carries the housing function, and the County Council which sits above it. Section 110 of the 2025 Act also requires local housing authorities (as well as any County Councils not having housing functions) to report to the Secretary of State on the exercise of their enforcement functions at such times and in such form as the Secretary of State requires.

Section 111 of the 2025 Act also enables the Secretary of State to appoint a 'lead authority', to take responsibility for those housing enforcement responsibilities which are delegated to it. That lead authority may be the Secretary of State or a separate agency appointed by the Secretary of State, which may include the Greater London Authority, a combined authority or a local housing authority. Section 112 describes the general duties and powers of the lead enforcement authority as being to oversee the operation of the provisions for which it is made responsible and to provide relevant local authorities, as well as the wider public, in England with advice and information about the operation of the provisions for which it is responsible.

Local housing authorities must also have regard to any guidance issued by the lead authority relating to their functions. Section 112(6) requires the lead authority to keep and review and from time to time advise the Secretary of State regarding the operation of the landlord provisions for which the lead authority is responsible as well as social and commercial developments relating to tenancies in England (other than tenancies of social housing),

So far as it considers those developments relevant matters for which is responsible, Section 113 empowers a lead authority to enforce the provisions for which it is responsible where it considers necessary or expedient to do so

DOI: 10.1201/9781003681403-7

and, for that purpose, to exercise any powers that a local housing authority may exercise for the enforcement of those provisions.

Where a lead authority proposes to take steps directly in respect of a breach or an offence under the provisions for which it is responsible, it must then notify the relevant local housing authority, which is then relieved of any duty to duplicate such action. Local housing authorities must also report to the lead authority when required to do so on the exercise of that local authority's functions under housing legislation

But note that those County Councils which do not have statutory housing functions are nonetheless empowered to enforce the new legislation, so far as relevant to their own statutory functions and provided also that the local housing authority is kept informed us to any proposed action on the part of the County Council, so as to avoid duplication

To help local housing authorities prepare for their enforcement duties under the new statutory regime, the MHCLG published on 13 November 2025, 10 pages of guidance titled, 'Enforcement of the New Tenancy System under The Renters' Rights Act 2025'. We have referred to this going forward as the Enforcement Guidance.

Running through the Enforcement Guidance is an expectation that councils will have already put in place detailed policies for enforcing the 2025 Act legislation before 1 May 2026 as well as advocating an aggressive approach towards enforcement of the new legislation. Councils are also incentivised to make full use of the civil penalties in preference to traditional prosecution, not only because in many cases it will involve a lower standard of proof and simpler administrative process, but also because councils will be able to recycle the income from those civil penalties towards the costs of enforcing the new regime, which, at least in theory, should be partly self-financing. The following paragraphs of the Enforcement Guidance would seem particularly relevant:

> There is no expectation that local housing authorities take informal steps to address the breach or offence. for example, by issuing warning letters, prior to taking formal action. Formal action includes issuing a statutory notice, such as an improvement notice, issuing a civil penalty notice or commencing prosecution proceedings. In determining what steps to take to address the breach or offence, local housing authorities should take account of the need for effective deterrence and punishment and what is in the best interests of tenants. Local Housing Authorities need to promptly follow up any actions to determine whether the non-compliance has ceased. Where any steps to end the non-compliance have failed to do so and the local housing authority is satisfied that the necessary evidential threshold is reached and proceeding is in the public interest, it <u>must</u> issue a civil penalty notice or start prosecution proceedings.

What this means for private landlords is that there will be no second chances in what is a very complex piece of legislation.

It is also important to mention at this stage that the new enforcement regime which took effect on 1 May 2026 will only apply to private landlords who are not registered social landlords. The same provisions will be applied to registered social landlords on a later date to be specified.

Section 107(1) of the 2025 Act states that it is the duty of every local housing authority to enforce the landlord legislation in its area. However, this does not prevent a local housing authority taking enforcement action in respect of an alleged contravention which has occurred outside its administrative area, provided that it keeps the other affected local authority notified of its intentions in so doing. In such cases, and to avoid duplication, that other local authority is then relieved of its duty to take enforcement action in relation to the same matter. For the purpose of these duties, 'landlord legislation' is defined to mean: Chapters 3 and 6 of Part 1 of the 2025 Act; Part 2 of the 2025 Act; Sections 1 1 and 1A of the Protection from Eviction Act 1977 and Chapter 1 of Part 1 of the 1988 Act.

To help local housing authorities enforce the new landlord duties, both as regards the requirement to issue to the tenant a Statement of Terms as well as the associated duties under the new Section 16E of the 1998 Act, Section 15 of the 2025 Act has introduced a new range of financial penalties as well as criminal offences. In summary, the options now available to a local housing authority to enforce the 2025 Act as well as associated housing legislation, includes:

1 The ability to prosecute
2 The ability to impose a range of financial penalties (either as an alternative to prosecution or in its own right)
3 Powerful investigation tools (see below)
4 An extension of existing powers contained in the Housing and Planning Act 2016 to apply for rent repayment orders (see below)
5 An extension of existing powers contained in the Housing and Planning Act 2016 to apply for banning orders (including entries on the Rogue Landlord Database)

Just to complicate matters, we mention that there are within the 2025 Act, three separate regimes empowering local authorities to impose financial penalties where there is a proven breach. Which financial penalty regime applies in any particular case depends on the particular section of the Act to which the breach applies. The first two regimes are set out in new Sections 16I to 16L of the 1988 Act as well as the insertion of a new Schedule 2ZA in the 1988 Act.

Financial penalties

We start with new Section 16I of the 1998 Act, which gives local housing authorities a discretion to impose civil financial penalties of up to £7,000 for non-compliance with the new landlord obligation to provide a Statement of Terms as well as for contravention of the other landlord duties referred to in Section 16E(1)(a)-(f). But the local housing authority can only impose a financial penalty if satisfied *beyond reasonable doubt* that the contravention has occurred.

A further qualification in that a financial penalty can only be imposed for a contravention of Section 16E(1)(e) [where landlord does not reasonably believe that they would be entitled to an order for possession on the specified grounds], in circumstances where the landlord achieved a surrender of the tenancy within four months from the day of that contravention and without a court order for possession of the premises having been made. Subsections (9) and (10) also empower the Secretary of State to give guidance to local housing authorities regarding the imposition of financial penalties and with a corresponding duty on local housing authorities to have due regard to such statutory guidance.

Criminal offences

A new Section 16J to the 1988 Act creates the following criminal offences, where in relation to an assured tenancy:

1. A person relies on a Schedule 2 ground for possession knowing that they would not be able to obtain a possession order on that ground or being reckless whether they would be able to do so and only in circumstances where, in reliance of the landlord's assertions, the tenant surrenders the tenancy within the following four months without court order for possession having been made. **Note** that the difference between this criminal offence and a breach of a landlord's Section 16E(1)(e) duty (see above – and which can only give rise to a financial penalty) is the amount of criminal intent required. For a prosecution to succeed under Section 16J(1), the prosecution must prove specific intent or recklessness. Liability to a civil penalty for breach of the Section 16E(1) requires only a lack of reasonable belief' that the ground for possession applies.
2. A person contravenes the 16E(2) or (3) prohibitions on marketing or letting within the 'restricted period', unless they can show that they took all reasonable steps to avoid that contravention.
3. An offence arises if, after a relevant financial penalty has been imposed and becomes final, the unlawful conduct for which the penalty was imposed, continues for the next 28 days or longer.
4. Where a person has conducted themselves in a manner giving rise to a financial penalty and within five years from the date on which that conduct occurs, a further penalty has been imposed on that person for different conduct, where that person has been convicted of an offence under this section for different conduct.

Note that a person cannot be prosecuted under Section 16J if a financial penalty had previously been imposed in respect of the same conduct. The maximum penalty for an offence under this section is a fine.

This brings us on to a new Section 16K of the 1988 Act, which enables a local housing authority to impose a financial penalty as an optional alternative to prosecution under Section 16J. This is separate from the power to impose financial penalties for less serious breaches of the landlord duties as referred to in Section 16I above. Nor does it appear to be an offer which a recipient landlord can choose to accept or reject. It is entirely within the discretion of the local housing authority whether to prosecute for Section 16J contravention or alternatively to impose a financial penalty of up to £40,000 in lieu.

The process of imposing financial penalties, whether under Sections 16I or 16K, is set out in the new Schedule 2ZA of the Housing Act 1988 (Financial penalties under Sections 16I and 16K), which can be summarised as follows:

- Step 1 – *Notice of intent.* The local housing authority must notify the recipient of its proposal to impose a financial penalty, which must be given within six months from the first day on which the authority has sufficient evidence of the conduct to which the financial penalty relates. This six-month time limit may be extended where conduct is continuing, until six months from the last day on which the conduct occurred. It is that Notice of Intent which must set out the amount of the proposed financial penalty and the reasons for imposing it and information about the recipient's right to make representations within the following 28 days.
- Step 2 – The local housing authority must consider any representations made by the recipient and then decide whether to impose a financial penalty, and if so, the amount of that penalty. If the authority still decides to impose a financial penalty, it must then issue a final notice requiring the penalty to be paid within 28 days from the issue of the notice. That final notice also gives information about the recipient's rights of appeal and the consequences of failure to comply with the notice.

Anyone receiving a final notice may appeal within 28 days to a first-tier tribunal, either against the decision to impose the penalty or against the amount of the penalty. If an appeal is made, the final notice is suspended pending the outcome of that appeal. Any appeal is to take the form of a re-hearing of the local housing authority's decision and may include matters of which the authority was previously unaware. Having heard an appeal, the first-tier tribunal may either confirm, reduce or cancel the final notice. Recovery of financial penalties is by the issue of proceedings in the county court. Once received a financial penalty may be applied towards meeting the council's costs and expenses in carrying out its enforcement functions either under this legislation or otherwise in relation to the private rented sector.

Paragraph 12 of the new Schedule 2ZA sets out the way that a local authority can use income received from these financial penalties. In short, a local housing authority may, at its discretion, apply such income towards meeting the costs and expenses (both administrative and legal) of the carrying out of its enforcement functions under the 2025 Act. Any penalty income *not* applied to meeting those costs and expenses must be paid across to the Secretary of State.

Section 57 of the 2025 introduces a new Section 1A to the Protection from Eviction Act 1977, which now enables a local housing authority to impose a financial penalty of up to £40,000 if satisfied beyond reasonable doubt that an offence involving unlawful eviction or harassment has been committed under Section 1 of the 1977 Act. This financial penalty may be imposed by the local authority as an alternative to prosecution under Section 1.

Finally, we turn to Section 99 and Schedule 5 of the 2025 Act (Financial Penalties), which introduced a third standalone tier of financial penalties for breach of Sections 40 [anti-discrimination], 57 [rental bidding], 66 [redress schemes] or 91 [marketing, advertising and letting].

Like the new Schedule 2ZA, as introduced into the 1988 Act for other financial penalties, Schedule 5 of the 2025 Act requires a Notice of Intent to be issued by the local housing authority within six months of the date of cessation of the prohibited conduct, which must also state the amount of the proposed penalty and the recipient's right to make representations to the issuer within the following 28 days. At the end of those 28 days, the authority must then decide whether to impose that financial penalty and, if it decides to do so, confirm the amount of that penalty. A final notice will then be issued to the person in default, requiring payment within the following 28 days. That final notice must set out: the date on which it was given; the amount of the financial penalty and the reasons for imposing that penalty; information about how to pay the penalty; the time for payment of the penalty; information about the recipient's rights of appeal and the consequences of failure to comply with the notice.

Anyone receiving a final notice may appeal within 28 days to the first-tier tribunal against either the decision to impose the penalty or the amount of the penalty and the final notice is suspended pending the outcome of that appeal. Once a penalty has become effective, the local housing authority may recover payment in the county court and may either utilise the proceeds towards the costs of its enforcement responsibilities or pay that sum to the Secretary of State.

Banning orders

Banning orders were introduced by Chapter 2 of Part 2 of the Housing and Planning Act 2016 and enable a first-year tribunal to ban a landlord from: letting housing in England; engaging in English letting work or engaging in English property management work. A banning order can only be made on the application of the local housing authority and only when the landlord has been convicted of one of the offences specified in the *Housing and Planning Act 2016 (Banning order Offences) Regulations 2018*. Those listed offences fall into either of the following two categories:

- Relevant housing offences – the listed offences include unauthorised eviction or harassment of a residential occupier as well as failure to comply with housing standards legislation.
- Other serious criminal offences – which include fraud; offences involving theft or violence; unauthorised drug use; antisocial behaviour as well as stalking/harassment offences.

Following conviction of one of the listed offences, the local housing authority can apply to the first-tier tribunal for the making of a Banning Order. Before doing so, the local authority must give the landlord at least 28 days prior written notice of its proposal to apply for the Banning Order, during which time the recipient landlord has an opportunity to make representations, which the local authority is obliged to consider before making the application. The first-tier tribunal then has power to make a Banning Order against a landlord or property agent who has been convicted a Banning Order offence and who was a landlord at the time the offence was committed. If granted, a Banning Order will last a minimum of 12 months and may be substantially longer. In deciding whether to make a Banning Order, the first-tier tribunal must also have regard to the sentence imposed by the court on the original conviction. There's no jurisdiction to make a Banning Order where the offender was given an absolute or conditional discharge by the criminal court. Nor can any account be taken of spent convictions. Contravention of a Banning Order is itself a criminal offence punishable by fine or imprisonment for up to 12 months.

When making a banning order, it is intended that the first-tier tribunal should draft the order in terms which protect the rights of existing tenants, and whose tenancies are not directly affected by the ban.

MHCLG Guidance to local authorities issued on 13 November 2025 and titled Banning Order Offences under the Housing and Planning Act 2016 contains the following advice to local authorities as regards publicity following the making of a Banning Order,

> *We would encourage local housing authorities to make successful banning orders for individual landlords public. They will wish to consider how to publish details of successful banning orders, including the names of individual landlords, at a local level.*

Note also Section 19 of the Housing and Planning Act 2016 which enables a local housing authority to require landlords to provide information to enable the local authority to decide whether to apply for a banning order. This could include requiring the landlord to provide information on all of the properties which the landlord owns. A landlord's failure, without reasonable excuse to provide information required is a criminal offence.

Management orders (interim and final)

Once a banning order has been made and where necessary to do so, a local housing authority can follow up with a management order in circumstances where a banning order has been made and where a privately rented property is being let in breach of that banning order. The power for local housing authorities to apply for management orders in those circumstances derives out of the Housing Act 2004 (as amended).

Making an interim management order in those circumstances does not require the local authority to make any further application to the first-tier tribunal. Once an Interim management order has been made, the local housing authority must ensure the health and safety of occupants at the property and others living or occupying property nearby. An interim management order also gives the local housing authority the following rights in relation to the property, including:

- A right to possession of the property subject to the rights of existing occupants.
- The rights of a landlord to collect rent, set rent levels, make repairs and manage the tenancies.
- Grant new tenancies or licenses with the consent of the landlord.

However, a management order does not enable a local housing authority to sell the property.

Making the management order means that the local housing authority will receive rent from the property in place of the landlord. That rental income may then be used to defray costs in managing the property and the ability to keep any surplus acquired during this period.

However, financial responsibility for paying any mortgage instalments associated with the property remains with the owner of that property. Nor does a management order prevent a mortgage lender from exercising any of their rights in respect to the property, including repossession. An interim management order can last up to 12 months from the date on which it is made.

At the end of an interim management order, the local authority can make a final management order if they are not satisfied that the health and safety of occupiers of the property and others living or owning nearby are protected. A final management order can last for up to five years. A landlord also has the ability to appeal to a first-tier tribunal against the making of an interim or final management order which appeal must be made within 28 days of the date the initial management order or final management order was made.

Rent repayment orders

Rent Repayment Orders (RROs) were introduced by the Housing and Planning Act 2016 and enable tenants and local authorities to receive up to two years worth of rent from a landlord who has committed certain housing related offences. Like banning orders, their purpose is to deter landlords from committing offences and also empowers tenants and local authorities to take action when a landlord acts illegally.

Like banning orders, see above, the power to apply for rent repayment orders is also dependent on the landlord having committed one of a specified list of offences, all of which are housing related. That list of offences has been extended by the 2025 Act to include: knowingly or recklessly misusing a possession ground; letting or marketing a property within 12 months of using the non-fault 'moving in' or 'selling' grounds of eviction or continuous breach of certain tenancy reform requirements. Note that unlike banning orders (see above), it is not necessary for the landlord to have actually been convicted of the offence providing the grounds for the rent repayment order.

Where grounds for an RRO exist, either the tenant or the local housing authority can apply to a first-tier tribunal for a RRO. However, the local authority can only make that application if at least part of the rent was paid through housing benefit or Universal Credit. If the tenant paid the whole of the rent from their own private resources, it is then only the tenant who can make the applications to the first-tier tribunal. Although proof of a criminal conviction is not required before a first-year tribunal can make an RRO, that tribunal still needs to be convinced beyond a reasonable doubt that an offence was actually committed. An RRO can only be applied for within two years of the date of the offence complained of. In some cases, the local housing authority and the tenant can apply jointly for an RRO. Another change brought about by the 2025 Act is that and RRO can also be made against a superior landlord who can be shown to have committed a housing related offence.

Application to a first-tier tribunal for a rent repayment order is made using Form RRO1. Before a local housing authority can apply to a first-tier tribunal for the making of a rent repayment order, it must first serve on the landlord or superior landlord a Notice of Intended Proceedings and give the recipient at least 28 days to make representations. Any representations received by the local housing authority must be given to due consideration before it proceeds further with its application. Notice of intended proceedings must be served within two years of the commission of the offence and explain why the local housing authority is proposing to apply an RRO and the amount it is seeking to recover.

More information about the making of rent repayment orders is contained in statutory guidance issued to local authorities on 13 November 2025 titled, Rent Repayment Orders: Guidance for Local Authorities. The fact that the guidance is expressed as being 'statutory' means that both local authorities and first-tier tribunals must have regard to it when making decisions associated with RROs. Examples of bad landlord conduct entitling a local authority to apply for an RRO include:

- Failure to make timely repairs, for instance: damp and mould, leaks, fire safety concerns, broken heating, pests
- Failure to provide the tenant with correct documentation at the start of the tenancy, such as: electrical and gas safety certificates, energy performance certificates, written statement of terms or tenancy agreements
- Fire hazards, such as: a lack of fire doors in an HMO, no smoke alarm, a key lock on the inside of the front door or bedroom door in an HMO as opposed to the safer thumb lock
- Harassment, aggression or intimidation, such as: attempting to evict the tenant without due process, entering the property without giving notice, raising the rent without following due process, threatening behaviour, other behaviour which could make the tenant vacate
- Non-compliance with other laws, possibly including: asking for or accepting a higher rent than as advertised, failure to give good reason for not allowing a pet, unlawful discrimination.

The statutory guidance also provides examples of good landlord conduct, including: responding to complaints and making acceptable repairs; providing all of the correct documents at the start of the tenancy and compliance with all other laws.

Where the first-tier tribunal makes a rent repayment order, recovery of money is through the county court. The statutory guidance also makes clear that the local housing authority can keep any surplus received through RROs, so long as it is used for functions relating to private rented sector enforcement activities.

8 New investigatory powers

To supplement local authority enforcement of the new landlord duties, as well as existing duties under the Protection from Eviction Act 1977 as amended and elsewhere, the government has conferred new investigatory powers on local housing authorities which took effect on 27 December 2025 and are explained below.

These new investigatory powers are contained in Part 4 Chapter 3 of the 2025 Act. They were also the first provisions of the 2025 Act, to take effect on 27 December 2025 in the expectation that the authorities will have enforcement policies in place by the time the main provisions of the Act took effect on 1 May 2026.

To assist local housing authorities in the use of the new investigatory powers, the Ministry of Housing, Communities and Local Government (MHCLG) published on 27 October 2025 its 'Investigatory Powers Guidance for Renters' Rights Act 2025'. This Guidance also warns housing offices that when using powers to require information under the 2025 Act, they must also comply with the Investigatory Powers Act 2016.

These new investigatory powers contain a complex mix of statutory provisions which enable authorised housing officials to demand information; seize documents; and enter premises, either with or without a justice's warrant. Some of these powers overlap, which means that housing officers sometimes have to exercise professional judgement when deciding the best power to use in particular circumstances, Whilst obstruction of a housing officer will in most circumstances be a criminal offence, that is not always the case, In at least one instance, enforcement is by way of application for an order from the county court to enforce compliance.

Section 114 – Power of local housing authority to require information from a *relevant person*

We start our review of investigatory powers with **Section 114** of the 2025 Act, which gives an authorised housing officer the power to give a written

DOI: 10.1201/9781003681403-8

notice to a ‘relevant person’, requiring them to provide requested information relating to any local authority function relating to legislation listed in Section 114(3) namely:

- Sections 1 and 1A of the Protection from Eviction Act 1977 (unlawful eviction and harassment)
- Chapter 1 of Part 1 of the Housing Act 1988 (assured tenancies)
- Section 83(1) or 84(1) of the Enterprise and Regulatory Reform Act 2013 (redress schemes for persons engaged in letting’s agency or property management)
- Sections 21–23 of the Housing and Planning Act 2016 (breach of banning order)
- Chapter 3 of Part 1 and Part 2 of this 2025 Act (discrimination and decent homes standard)

Section 114 can only be used to require information from a ‘relevant person’, which is defined by Section 114(2) to mean anyone (other than a mortgage lender) whom within the preceding 12 months has had a proprietary interest in ‘relevant accommodation’ or has been involved in the licensing or marketing of that accommodation. ‘Relevant Accommodation’ is defined by Section 114(10) as being any residential accommodation in England which is connected with the exercise or proposed exercise of a function in relation to which the investigatory power is exercised.

Unlike Section 115 below, the use of the Section 114 power does not require any reasonable suspicion that the law has been broken by anyone but is simply to assist the local housing authority in carrying out the legislative functions to which Section 114 refers. However, use of the Section 111 power to require information is subject to the following limitations:

- It can only be used to require the provision of information from a ‘relevant person’ (see above);
- A notice issued under Section 114 cannot require a recipient to provide any information or create any documents which could be refused in civil proceedings on the grounds of legal professional privilege.

As to process, any notice requiring information under this Section 114 must be in writing and specify it is given under Section 114. The notice may also specify the time within which and the manner in which the information is to be provided. The notice may also require the creation of documents and the provision of those documents to the enforcement authority but must include information about the possible consequences of not complying with a Section 114 notice. Those consequences can include prosecution of an offence under Section 131 of the 2025 Act (see below). There is also a general protection against self-incrimination (Section 131(6))

Section 115: Power of local housing authority to require information from *any person*

In one respect, the Section 115 power to require information is wider than the Section 114 power outlined above, in that it can be used to require information from anyone not only a 'relevant person' (as defined above). But the corresponding limitation of Section 115 is that a housing officer can only use it to obtain information if they reasonably suspect that has been a breach of or an offence under the 'rented accommodation legislation', which is defined as follows:

- Sections 1 and 1A of the Protection from Eviction Act 1977 (unlawful eviction and harassment)
- Chapter 1 of Part 1 of the Housing Act 1988 (assured tenancies)
- Parts 1–4 and 7 of the Housing Act 2004 so far as relating to 'Qualifying Residential Premises', as defined by Section 2B of that Act (housing standards)
- Section 83(1) or 84(1) of the Enterprise and Regulatory Reform Act 2013 (redress schemes for persons engaged in lettings agency or property management)
- Sections 21–23 of the Housing and Planning Act 2016 (breach of banning order)
- Chapter 3 of Part 1 and Part 2 of this 2025 Act (discrimination and decent homes standard)

This list is wider than the corresponding list contained in Section 114(3) above, in its inclusion of Parts 1–4 and 7 of the Housing Act 2004 so far as relating to 'Qualifying Residential Premises', as defined by Section 2B of that Act (housing standards)

When Section 115 applies, it allows an authorised local housing officer to give written notice to anyone, requiring that person to provide the local housing authority or that officer with the information specified in that notice. Any notice given under this Section 115 *may* specify the time and the manner in which the recipient must comply with it and the form in which the information must be provided. The notice may also require the creation of specified documents and the provision of those documents to an enforcement authority or officer. The notice must also include information about the possible consequences of non-compliance.

In the event of a recipient's failure to comply with a notice requiring information, Section 116 of the 2025 Act allows the enforcement authority to apply to the High Court or a county court for an order to force compliance, and the terms of that court order may also require the person in default to meet the costs related to that application. A court order issued under Section 116 can require the defaulting party to do anything that the court thinks is reasonable for that person to do for any of the purposes for which the original notice was given and to ensure that it is complied with. Where the party in default is a company, partnership or an unincorporated association, the court may require any director, manager, or member of that organisation who is responsible for the failure, to meet the costs of the application. It must also be assumed that any subsequent failure by the person responsible to comply with the order could be punished as a contempt of court.

To avoid the possibility of self-incrimination, Section 117 of the 2025 Act protects the person providing information under Section 115 against the use of that information in any subsequent criminal proceedings against that person. However, that does not prevent the person providing that information from making reference to it in any criminal proceedings. The protection against use of that information in criminal proceedings does not, on the face of it, prevent the use of that information in any civil proceedings in that respect. The exemption must be contrasted with the exemption for information covered by legal professional privilege referred to in Section 114. **Note** also that the protection from self-incrimination does not cover offences under Section 5 Perjury Act 1911 (false statutory declarations and other false statements without oath), where someone knowingly or wilfully provides false information, either in a written format or orally, where such information is required in pursuance of a statutory obligation.

Section 118: Business premises: entry without warrant

Section 118 of the 2025 Act allows an officer of a local housing authority at any reasonable time to enter premises in England if the officer first reasonably believes those premises to be occupied by a 'relevant person' for the purposes of a 'rental sector business' and second that the officer considers it necessary to enter the premises to exercise powers under Section 122 or Section 123 below for purposes connected with any function of the authority under or by virtue of the 'rented accommodation legislation'. However, Section 118 does not authorise entry into any premises used wholly or mainly as residential accommodation.

Section 118 then distinguishes between what is termed a 'routine inspection' and those inspections regarded as 'non-routine'. The distinction between the two types of inspection is crucial as it is only in relation to 'routine inspections' that the officer is required under Section 118(3) to give at least 24 hours prior written notice of that intended inspection to an occupier of the premises. That advance notice must also set out why entry is considered necessary and that obstructing the carrying out of the inspection can constitute an offence under Section 131 of the 2025 Act (see below). All inspections will be regarded as 'routine' unless the housing officer reasonably considers that the giving of notice would defeat the purpose of the entry or where it is not reasonably practicable in all the circumstances to give such notice. The requirement to give 24 hours prior written notice also does not apply if any occupier of the premises has waived the need for notice to be given. Subsections 118(7) and (8) allow a housing officer entering premises to be accompanied by such other personnel as the officer thinks necessary and enables the officer to take photographs or make recordings. Subsection 118(9) defines a 'rental sector business', as being a business connected with:

1 The letting of residential accommodation in England
2 The creation of licences to occupy residential accommodation
3 The marketing of residential accommodation for the purpose of creating a tenancy or occupational licence
4 The management of residential accommodation when occupied under a tenancy or occupational licence

Section 119 (duties where occupiers are on business premises entered without a warrant), supplements the Section 118 power of entry by requiring the officer to produce evidence of their identity and authority to anyone present and in the event of a non-routine inspection, to provide that occupant with a document explaining why the entry is necessary and explaining the Section 131(1) and (2) offences if entry is obstructed. However, an officer is not required to comply with these requirements if it is not reasonably practicable to do so. Nor does a failure to comply with the identity and authority requirements of itself nullify any later proceedings brought in circumstances where the entry is obstructed.

Section 120: Business premises: warrant authorising entry

Section 120 enables a housing officer to apply on oath to a justice of the peace for a warrant authorising entry to business premises (using reasonable force if necessary) on any of the following grounds:

1 The officer would, in entering the premises, be acting in the course of their employment by, or on, the instructions of the local housing authority.
2 There are reasonable grounds for believing that:

    i the premises are occupied by a relevant person for the purposes of a rental sector business (see above);
    ii the premises are not used wholly or mainly as residential accommodation;
    iii on the premises, there are documents which the local housing authority can require someone to produce under Section 122 or seize under Section 123 (below) and
    iv Condition A, B or C (below) is met.

Condition A will apply where access to the premises has been or is likely to be refused, and notice of the local housing authority's intention to apply for a warrant has been given to an occupier of the premises.

Condition B will apply when it is likely that documents on the premises would be concealed or interfered with if notice of entry was given to an occupier of the premises.

Condition C will apply if there is no occupier present, and it might defeat the purpose of the entry to await their return.

It is for the justice of the peace to whom the application is made, to be satisfied on all of these points before issuing a warrant authorising entry under Section 120.

Section 121: Business premises; entry under warrant

Section 121 deals with the manner in which any warrant issued under Section 120 above is to be executed. The authorised officer may enter into the premises at any reasonable time during the period of one month following the issue of the warrant and using reasonable force if necessary. But it cannot authorise entry into premises used wholly or mainly as residential accommodation. The authorised officer may also be accompanied by such persons as that officer thinks necessary and that officer may also take photographs or make recordings. If there is anyone present on the premises when the entry is effected, the officer must produce their warrant for inspection to at least one of those occupants

In the event that there is no occupier present when the entry is effected, the officer must leave a notice on the premises stating that they have been entered under a warrant and also leave the premises as effectively secured against trespassers as the officer found them.

Section 122: Power to require production of documents following entry

An authorised housing officer who has entered premises either with or without a warrant under Sections 118 or 120 at any reasonable time may also require a 'relevant person' occupying the premises or anyone acting on behalf of that person, to produce any documents relating to the 'relevant business' to which that person has access and also authorises the officer to take copies of that document or entry in that document. However an authorised officer can only require production of documents and the opportunity to take copies to enable the officer to ascertain whether there has been compliance with the 'rented accommodation legislation' in circumstances where the local housing authority reasonably suspects a breach of that legislation or the commission of an offence and to ascertain whether the documents may be required as evidence in proceedings for such a breach or offence.

It does not matter whether the suspected breach or offence relates to the 'relevant person' or to someone else. The power to require production of documents also includes a housing officer's right to insist that the person producing the document explains the document.

Where a document contains information recorded electronically, the officer can require production of a copy of that document in a form which can be easily taken away and which is visible and legible. Section 122 also reserves the right of anyone to refuse to produce a document which that person would be entitled to withhold in proceedings in the High Court on the grounds of legal professional privilege. In this Section 122, 'relevant business' means the business for the purposes of which the premises are occupied.

Section 123: Power to seize documents following entry

Running alongside the Section 122 power enabling officers to require production of documentation and the ability to take copies, is this Section 123, which enables that officer to seize and detain documents which that officer reasonably suspects may be required as evidence in proceedings relating to a breach of the 'rented accommodation legislation' or an offence under that legislation.

Where premises are occupied at the time of such seizure, the officer must provide to at least one of those occupants, evidence of the officer's identity and authority before seizing the documentation, but only to the extent that it is reasonably practicable to do so. When seizing documentation under this Section 123, the officer must also take reasonable steps to inform the person from whom the documentation is seized, that it has been seized and provide that person with a written record of what has been seized. In determining what steps have to be taken as regards informing the person from whom they documentation is seized, the officer must have regard to the provisions of any Code of Practice made under Section 66 of the Police and Criminal Evidence Act 1984.

One such Code of Practice is Section 7 (Seizure and Retention of Property), of the Police and Criminal Evidence Act 1984 Code B revised, titled, '*Code of practice for Searches of Premises by Police Officers and the Seizure of Property found by police officers on persons or premises*'. Although this Code of practice is expressed to apply to searches and seizure of property by police officers, it is applied here by analogy to searches and seizure by authorised housing officers under Section 123 of the Renters' Rights Act 2025.

The powers of seizure contained in Section 123 are also expressed to extend to access to any electronic device on which information may be stored or from which it may be accessed. Documentation seized under this Section 123 may not be detained for more than three months beginning on the date of the seizure but may be detained for longer if required for the purposes of proceedings for which they were seized.

It may be necessary for a housing officer to apply to a justice of the peace under Section 120 of the 2025 Act for a warrant authorising entry (using reasonable force if necessary) in any of the following circumstances:

- Access to the premises has been or is likely to be refused where notice of the local housing authorities intention to apply for a warrant has previously been given to an occupier of the premises.
- It is considered likely that documents on the premises would be concealed or interfered with if prior written notice of entry were given to an occupier of the premises.
- There is no occupier present, and it might defeat the purpose to delay the entry for their return.

In the event that there is no occupier present when the entry is effected, the housing officer must leave a notice on the premises stating that they have been entered under a warrant and also leave the premises as effectively secured against trespassers as the officer found them.

Section 122 of the 2025 Act enables the housing officer to require production of documents following entry and to take copies of any such documents for the purposes of ascertaining whether there has been compliance with rented accommodation legislation. Section 123 also allows a housing officer to seize documents following entry but only if the officer reasonably suspects that they may be required as evidence in relation to rented accommodation legislation.

Section 124: Access to seized documents

This section allows the person from whom documentation was seized, to request access to that document, which may include a request for a photograph or copy of the document. On receipt of such a request, the local housing authority must allow such access or the taking of a photograph or copy, under the supervision of an officer. However, access to the document or copying facilities can be refused if the local housing authority has reasonable grounds for believing that to allow access or copying would undermine the purposes for which the documentation was seized. The request for access may come either from the person from whom the document was seized or alternatively from someone representing that person. Section 124(6) allows the local housing authority to recover its reasonable cost in complying with a request for access to documentation under this section.

Section 125: Appeal against detention of documents

Where documentation has been seized by the local housing authority in relation to this legislation, Section 125 allows anyone having an interest in that documentation to apply to the magistrates court for an order releasing that documentation.

Where proceedings for an alleged offence are already in progress, the application must be made to the magistrates as part of those proceedings. But if there are no criminal proceedings currently in progress, the aggrieved make a stand-alone 'complaint' to a magistrates court. Where an application is made for release of documentation under this Section 125, a magistrates court can only order such release if satisfied that either of the following conditions, A or B, has been met.

Condition A will apply either where no proceedings have been brought for an offence connected with the investigation for which the documents were seized, or alternatively, that more than six months from the date of seizure has now expired.

Condition B will apply where proceedings for an offence have been brought and those proceedings have been concluded.

There is a general right of appeal to the Crown Court from a decision of the magistrates court either authorising release of the documentation or refusing release. Any order of the magistrates court under this Section 125 may also contain provisions suspending its operation pending the outcome of any appeal to the Crown Court.

Section 126: Suspected residential tenancy: entry without warrant

This Section 126 allows a specially authorised housing officer to enter premises in England at any reasonable time if that officer reasonably suspects that the premises or any part of the premises are subject to a 'residential tenancy', as defined by Section 63(1) of the 2025 Act (which excludes social housing). In other words, it is a residential tenancy operated by a private landlord. Furthermore, such tenancies are not limited to assured tenancies under the 1988 Act but may also include a regulated tenancy within the meaning of the Rent Act 1977. The prime purpose of that entry must be to enable the housing officer to identify whether there are premises which should be registered in the landlord database or which are being let in breach a Banning Order or where there are suspected offences relating to those requirements.

The housing officer proposing to affect entry under this Section 126 must first serve not less than 24 hours prior written notice on the occupier of the premises as well as anyone else having a proprietary interest in the premises other than a 'residential landlord'; a mortgagee or someone who has waived the need for such a notice. Any notice of intended entry issued under this Section 126 must explain why the entry is considered necessary and the penal consequences of obstruction.

In circumstances where no prior notice is given, the housing officer must issue such notice within a reasonable time following the entry. Any notice issued after the event must identify the premises which were entered, state when the premises were entered, and the purpose for which the premises were entered. A specially authorised housing officer entering premises under this section may be accompanied by other people and take onto the premises such equipment as the officer thinks necessary, including the taking of photographs or the making of recordings.

Section 127: Duties where occupiers are on residential premises entered without warrant

This Section 127 supplements the Section 126 power of entry by requiring the specially authorised housing officer to produce evidence of their identity and special authorisation to an occupier present on the premises or if there is more than one occupier, to at least one of those occupiers. However, the officer is only required to do this to the extent that it is practicable to do so. Nor are any proceedings consequent on the Section 126 inspection invalidated because of a failure by the officer to provide evidence of Identity and authorisation.

Section 128: Suspected residential tenancy: warrant authorising entry

This Section 128 enables a justice of the peace to issue a warrant authorising a named local housing authority officer to enter premises in England as specified in the warrant if satisfied, following information given on oath that the following conditions are satisfied:

a That the officer would, in entering the premises, be acting in the course of their employment and on the instructions of the local housing authority.
b That there are reasonable grounds to suspect that the whole or part of the premises is subject to a residential tenancy as defined by Section 63.
c That it is necessary for the officer to inspect the premises to investigate whether there has been a breach or an offence relating to the landlord database or a banning order.
d That admission to the premises has been sought but refused; that no occupant is present and it might defeat the purpose of the entry to await their return; or that application for admission would defeat the purpose of the inspection.

Section 129: Suspected residential tenancy: entry under warrant

This Section 129 supplements warrant entry under Section 128 by making clear that the officer can enter at any reasonable time and using reasonable force if necessary and that the warrant ceases to have effect when the inspection of the premises has been completed. Section 129(3) also enables the officer to be accompanied by other people and to take photographs or make recordings. The warrant must also be produced for inspection to any occupants found on the premises or at least one of those occupants. If no one is found on the premises when the entry takes place, the officer must leave a notice on the premises stating that they have been entered under warrant under Section 128 and leave the premises as effectively secured against trespass as when the officer entered those premises.

Section 130: Power of accompanying persons

This Section 130 extends the warrant powers to anyone else accompanying the authorised housing officer, save that the other person can only exercise those powers in the company of and under the supervision of the authorised officer.

Section 131: Offences

Section 131 makes it an offence for anyone without reasonable excuse to obstruct an authorised local housing officer who is exercising or seeking to exercise any power to require information or enter premises in accordance with the powers conferred by this Chapter 3 of Part 4 of the 2025 Act (Investigatory Powers). The only exception is in relation to the Section 115 power of an authorised housing officer (who reasonably suspects a breach of the rented accommodation legislation) to require anyone to provide specified information.

A breach of Section 115 cannot lead prosecution but may instead lead to an application by the housing officer to the county court for an order requiring the disclosure of the specified information, Section 115(2) makes it an offence for anyone to knowingly or recklessly give information to an authorised housing officer which is false or misleading in a material respect. Section 131(3) makes it a criminal offence for someone to pretend to be an officer of a local housing authority in relation to the exercise of any of these powers. The maximum penalty for an offence under this Section 131 is a fine of up to level 3 on the standard scale [£1,000]. Section 131(6) restates the fact that no one can be required to answer any question or give information which might incriminate that person.

Section 132: Investigatory powers: interpretation

Section 132 lists out a series of definitions relevant to these investigatory powers. Section 132(4) makes clear that the duties and powers conferred on an authorised housing officer under this Chapter 3 of Part 4 of the 2025 Act are not intended to authorise the processing of information which would contravene Data Protection Legislation or Parts 1–7 of the Investigatory Powers Act 2016.

Sections 133–136 (Amendments)

The MCHLG guidance issued to local authorities on the 27 October 2025 in relation to the use of investigatory powers, emphasised that the new statutory powers introduced by Chapter 3 of Part 4 of the 2025 Act (Iinvestigatory Powers), are not intended to be stand-alone but are to be read together with investigatory powers already contained in other legislation, including, in particular, the Housing Act 2004 and the Housing and Planning Act 2016. These sections also make amendments to those other investigatory powers to cater for the new duties on local authorities imposed by the 2025 Act.

Sections 133–136 of the 2025 Act deal with those amendments and are summarised below. These sections must be read together with other legislation which assist authorised housing officers carrying out their duties to investigate breaches of relevant landlord legislation and which includes the following.

1 An amendment made by Section 134 of the 2025 Act to Section 212A of the Housing Act 2004, which will enable the Secretary of State to require the operators of tenancy deposit schemes to share information with local housing authorities to support the enforcement of the following legislation: Sections 1 and 1A of the Protection from Eviction Act 1977 (unlawful eviction and harassment); Housing Act 1988 Chapter 1 of Part 1 (assured tenancies); Sections 83(1) or 84(1) of the Enterprise and Regulatory Reform Act 2013 (redress schemes relevant to letting and property management work); Chapter 1 of Part I of the Housing Act 2004 (housing standards);' Section 21–23, 41 and 133 to 135 of the Housing and Planning and Parts 1 and 2 of the 2025 Act (tenancy reform and residential landlords).
2 An amendment made by the same Section 134 extends Section 237 of the Housing Act 2004 (Use of housing benefit and Council tax information for other statutory purposes) to a local authority's functions under Part 7 of that 2004 Act to qualifying residential premises within the meaning given by Section 2B of that Act as well as Sections 1 and 1A of the Protection from Eviction Act 1977 (unlawful eviction and harassment); Housing Act 1988 chapter 1 of part 1 (assured tenancies); Sections 83(1) or 84(1) of the Enterprise and Regulatory Reform Act 2013 (redress schemes relevant to letting and property management work); Chapter 1 of Part I of the Housing Act 2004 (housing standards) Section 21–23, 41 and 133–135 of the Housing and Planning Act 2016 and Parts 1 and 2 of the 2025 Act (tenancy reform and residential landlords).

3 Section 135 of the 2025 Act extends Section 235 of the Housing Act 2004 (power to require documents to be produced), to a purpose connected with the exercise of any local authority function in relation to 'qualifying residential premises', as defined by Section 2B of the Housing Act 2004. This change means that officers can now require information from a relevant person to inform the setting of civil penalties after investigations have been finished.

4 Section 136 of the 2025 Act extends paragraph 10 Schedule 5 of the Consumer Rights Act 2015 (Duties and powers to which schedule 5 applies) to investigations relating to regulations 5 and 8 of the Client Money Protection Schemes for Property Agents (Requirement to belong to a scheme, etc.) Regulations 2019 This means that enforcement authorities can now investigate whether an agent is a member of a client money protection scheme.

9 Anti-discrimination and pets

Anti-discrimination in relation to the lettings market, on grounds of race, sex and other protected characteristics already exists in the form of the Equality Act 2010, Chapter 3 of Part 1 of the 2025 Act now extends these anti-discrimination provisions to include benefits status and financial circumstances in the context of residential letting. The 2025 Act now contains express provisions to prevent discrimination in the residential lettings market against tenants or prospective tenants who either:

- have, or will have, children living with them or visiting them at the premises or
- will be in receipt of benefits.

In each case, the outlawing of such discrimination is not absolute and may be allowed to the extent that it can be shown to be a proportionate means of achieving a legitimate aim. Such discrimination may also be permitted where it would put the landlord, their agent or a superior landlord in breach of an existing insurance policy which prohibits a tenant from having a child living with or visiting them at the dwelling or prevents the tenant from having a certain benefit status. This insurance exception will only apply if the offending terms in that insurance policy are not rendered ineffective by Section 37 of the 2025 Act, which invalidates any insurance requirement that prevents a tenant from having a child living with them or visiting them or alternatively prevents the tenant from being a benefits claimant.

However, the neutralisation of these insurance conditions will not apply to insurance contracts in existence on 1st May 2026, the date Section 37 took effect, but will apply to any extension or renewal of that policy. **Note** in particular that reference to 'benefits' is not limited to means-tested benefits but is widely drawn to include payments under the Social Security Contributions and Benefits Act 1992, The Welfare Reform Act 2012; Job Seekers Act 1995, State Pension Credit Act 2002, Tax credits Act 2002, Welfare Reform Act 2007 and Pensions Act 2014. The reference to benefits recipients also includes anyone who qualifies for a reduction of council tax under Section 13A of

DOI: 10.1201/9781003681403-9

the Local Government Finance Act 1992. As would be expected, a child is defined as someone under the age of 18. We now turn to the detail of these anti-discrimination provisions and how they are enforced.

To assist local housing authorities in their responsibilities for enforcing these anti-discrimination revisions, the MHCLG published guidance on 13 November 2025 titled *Rental Discrimination under the Renters' Rights Act 2025*. For ease of reference, we have throughout this section referred to it as the Discrimination Guidance. As will be seen, these anti-discrimination provisions will apply to any assured tenancy other than those tenancies granted by registered social landlords or which are of supported accommodation.

Throughout these anti-discrimination provisions, a 'relevant person' is defined by Section 42(1) of the 2025 Act to be either a prospective landlord or someone who is acting directly or indirectly on behalf of a prospective landlord. The Discrimination Guidance also suggests that reference to someone acting indirectly on behalf of a prospective landlord could extend to a family member acting on their behalf. But these provisions cannot place any responsibilities on someone who does nothing more than publishing an advertisement, other than as part of a letting business, The other key definition for the purposes of Chapter 3 is a 'relevant tenancy', which Section 42(1) defines to mean an assured tenancy *other than a tenancy of social housing or supported accommodation.*

We begin with Section 33 of the 2025 Act which prevents discrimination against someone with children (or to whom children may visit), when making premises available for letting on a 'relevant tenancy'. It is now unlawful for a 'relevant person' to prevent that prospective tenant from enquiring whether the dwelling is available to let; from accessing information about the dwelling or viewing it; or entering into a tenancy of the dwelling. It is also unlawful for that 'relevant person' to apply any provision, criterion or practice to make it less likely that the prospective tenant would enter into a tenancy of that dwelling.

Section 34 provides similar anti-discrimination provisions as Section 33 above but in relation to a prospective tenant who is in receipt of benefits.

Section 35 of the 2025 Act deals with the situation where it is the tenancy agreement itself which contains terms prohibiting the tenant from having a child live with or visit them or restricting the circumstances in which that may happen. Any such contractual provision is now declared void, save to the extent that it is a proportionate means of achieving a legitimate aim or if the insurance exception applies. Section 35 similarly disapplies any contractual provisions which discriminate against benefit claimants.

Section 36 deals with superior leases and declares void any term of that lease either preventing a tenant having a child living with them or visiting them or subletting to a benefits claimant. Again, there are exceptions for legitimate aims or to avoid infringing the terms of an insurance policy.

Section 37 declares void the terms of any mortgage which prevent the mortgagor letting to someone having a child living or visiting them at the dwelling or from letting to a benefits claimant.

Section 38 (as previously referred to) declares void any discriminatory provisions against tenants with children or benefits payments, contained in any insurance policy which is either entered into, extended or renewed after the date these changes came into force.

Section 39 of the 2025 Act enables the Secretary of State to make regulations extending the rules against discrimination in letting, to other protected groups.

Section 40 of the 2025 Act gives local housing authorities the task of enforcing the Chapter 3 anti-discrimination provisions through the use of financial penalties up to £7,000, with the prospect of repeat penalties where conduct continues after 28 days. Unlike the financial penalties previously referred where landlords are shown to have acted unlawfully and which require proof beyond reasonable doubt, when it comes to enforcement of the anti-discrimination provisions, it is sufficient if the local housing authority is satisfied on the balance of probabilities that someone has acted in a discriminatory way as regards prospective tenants with children or who are in receipt of benefits.

Finally, Section 41 of the 2025 Act makes clear that nothing in these anti-discrimination provisions prevents a landlord from taking a prospective tenant's income into account when considering whether that person would be able to afford the rent payable under that tenancy. However, the Discrimination Guidance makes clear that when assessing the income of a prospective tenant, income derived from benefits must be given equal status to other earned or unearned income. Nor can any of these financial tests be structured in a way which indirectly discriminates against families with children or benefit recipients. The Discrimination Guidance also warns that it would not be acceptable for a landlord to refuse a prospective tenant in receipt of benefits because rent guarantee insurance is denied to the landlord because that prospective tenant is a benefits claimant.

Whilst these new statutory provisions allow discrimination which is both proportionate and in pursuance of a legitimate aim, it is important to know what types of discriminatory conduct would be considered acceptable in this context. The Discrimination Guidance provides the following examples of discriminatory conduct which might be considered proportionate and legitimate:

- A retirement home or student accommodation
- Premises which might be unsafe for small children
- Possibly a restrictive covenant in a freehold title deed (but not in a superior lease, mortgage or insurance policy).

However, these examples are not blanket exemptions. It might still be disproportionate to prevent someone with a child from visiting a retirement complex. And premises which might be unsafe for smaller children may still be safe for an adolescent. The key issue in each of these cases is that any discriminatory practice can only be considered proportionate and in pursuance of a legitimate aim if it benefits someone other than the landlord. In the case of a retirement complex, the beneficiaries of such a restriction might be the other retirees resident in the complex.

Right to request permission to keep a pet

The new standalone Sections 16(A) to 16(C) to the 1988 Act, as introduced by Section 11 of the 2025 Act, *do not* give an assured tenant the right to keep a pet in circumstances where the tenancy agreement restricts the keeping of pets. It merely gives the assured tenant a statutory right to request that the landlord grants permission for the keeping of a pet, even where the tenancy agreement absolutely prohibits the keeping of pets. In that respect, the new Sections 16(A) to (C) override any contractual provision to the contrary contained in the tenancy agreement. The new provisions only have relevance where, as will usually be the case, the tenancy agreement contains restrictions on the keeping of pets or particular types of pet.

Whether or not permission is granted for the keeping of a particular pet is for the landlord to decide, save as regards a new statutory obligation on a landlord to act reasonably in deciding whether to grant or refuse consent for the keeping of that pet. A landlord who is minded to grant such consent may also set the terms on which that consent is granted. It follows that landlords must deal with each application on a case-by-case basis and be clear as to their reasons if consent is refused. We now look in more detail at the relevant statutory provisions regarding a tenant's request to keep a pet:

1 A new Section 16A to the 1988 Act makes it an implied term of every assured tenancy (except a tenancy of social housing), that a tenant may keep a pet at the tenanted premises if the landlord permits the tenant to do so and that such consent cannot be unreasonably refused.
The provisions would seem to cover an animal of any description which the tenant requires as a matter of personal interest; companionship or for ornamental purposes, 16C(2).

3 A tenant's request to keep a pet must be made in writing and contain a description of the pet for which consent is sought, 16B(3).

4 Once a valid application has been received, the landlord must give their response, granting or refusing the request, within 28 days. However, the 28-day time limit may be extended when the landlord reasonably requests further information about the particular pet. Where further information is requested, the 28-day time limit is extended until the expiration of seven days from which the further information is provided. If that information is not provided, the landlord is no longer required to respond to that request.

5 The 28-day time limit is also extended in circumstances where the immediate landlord has to apply to a superior landlord before consenting to the tenant's request.
6 It is deemed reasonable for an immediate landlord to refuse consent if a superior lease under which the landlord holds its interest, absolutely prohibits the keeping of pets. However, if the superior tenancy gives the superior landlord a discretion to allow the keeping of a pet, the immediate landlord under the assured tenancy must take reasonable steps to seek the consent of the superior landlord.
7 The right to request permission to keep a pet does not apply to assured tenancies of social housing.
8 Where a landlord fails to comply with its obligations in relation to regulated pet requests, it would seem that a tenant's primary recourse is for an order of specific performance through the county court, as a breach of the tenancy on the part of the landlord (Section 16B(5)).

10 Landlord registration and housing standards

Registration

Houses in multiple occupation (HMOs) are already the subject of statutory registration schemes under the Housing Act 2004. But it is Local Housing Authorities who are individually responsible for licensing and registering HMOs in their areas. Added to this is the Rogue Landlord Register which, nationwide, has scarcely a couple of hundred names recorded on it. The only register open to public access, at the time of writing, is the non-statutory *Rogue Landlord and Agent Checker* maintained by the Greater London Authority. But that is expected to change in late 2026 when the Government implements Chapter 3 of Part 2 of the 2025 Act, which involves the establishment of the *Private Rented Sector Database*.

As its name suggests, the new database will only relate to private landlords and not those in the social rented sector.

Section 73 of the 2025 Act requires the 'database operator', meaning either the Secretary of State or another organisation appointed by the Secretary of State, to establish and operate a database containing, first, entries in respect of persons who are or who intend to become residential landlords ('landlord entries') and second, entries in relation to dwellings which are or are intended to be let under residential tenancies ('dwelling entries'). Entries will also be made in relation to persons against whom Banning Orders have been made or who have been subject to prosecution or penalties or other regulatory action. New regulations will set out how the database is to work and for the need for active entries to be kept up to date. Landlords and their agents may also be charged fees for entry onto the database.

Key to the new registration regime is Section 82 of the 2025 Act (restrictions on marketing, advertising and letting dwellings), which will make it illegal for anyone to market a dwelling for the purpose of creating a residential tenancy unless there is an active landlord entry in the database as well as an active dwelling entry in the database. It will also be a requirement for anyone advertising such a dwelling, in any written advertisement, to include unique database identifiers for the person who will be the residential landlord as well

DOI: 10.1201/9781003681403-10

as for the dwelling. However, Section 82(5) protects the rights of any tenant as regards the validity or enforceability of a residential tenancy, which is granted in breach of the registration requirements.

Section 83 requires local housing authorities to make entries in the database in respect of relevant banning orders, convictions as well as any financial penalty imposed in relation to a relevant banning order offence. A local housing authority also has a discretion to put an entry in the database in relation to successful prosecutions or financial penalties imposed by someone other than the local housing authority. Section 84 of the 2025 Act states that the database operator must allocate a unique identifier to each person as well as each dwelling for which an entry is made in the database. In setting up the database, the database operator is also required:

- To ensure that facilities are available for persons unable to use a computer or other electronic device or who do not wish to do so to make and maintain landlord entries and dwelling entries in the database.
- To ensure that local housing authorities are able to edit the database for the purpose of carrying out the functions conferred on them.
- To ensure that facilities are available for breaches of the Section 82 registration requirement to be reported to the database operator and passed on to such local housing authorities as the database operator thinks appropriate.
- To publish advice and information explaining to residential landlords and residential tenants the rights and obligations as regards registration.
- To report to the Secretary of State on the performance of the database or the emerging trends relating to the database and information contained in it, that the database operator considers should be brought to the attention of the Secretary of State.

It is clear from Section 86 that the new database is *not* intended to be publicly accessible and will provide access to information *only* to the following: lead enforcement authorities, local housing authorities, English weights and measures authorities, mayoral combined authorities and the Greater London Authority. Section 87 prohibits unauthorised disclosure of restricted information from the database.

Section 86 makes clear that a lead enforcement authority or a local housing authority may only use information obtained from the database for purposes connected with their respective functions relating to housing, presidential landlords or residential tenancies.

Section 89 requires the database operator to remove a landlord or dwelling entry from the database if it has been an inactive entry for a continuous period of five years. That is extended to ten years for entries relating to banning orders, offences or financial penalties.

Key to the enforceability of the registration requirement is Section 90 of the 2025 Act which prevents a court from granting possession of a dwelling house on any ground (other than the Ground 7A or 14 antisocial behaviour grounds), if the landlord is in breach of any registration requirement relating to that dwelling house. Anyone who markets or lets a residential dwelling without having complied with Section 82 of the 2025 Act may be required to pay a financial penalty of up to £7,000. For an offence under Section 92 of the 2025 Act, that penalty rises to a maximum of £40,000 (see below).

Section 92 of the 2025 Act makes it an offence for anyone knowingly or recklessly to provide information to the database which is false or misleading in a material respect. It is also an offence if unlawful conduct continues more than 28 days after a financial penalty has been imposed or if within five years, there is other illegal conduct.

Section 93 empowers the Secretary of State from time to time to give directions to the database operator as well as local housing authorities about how they are to carry out their functions as regards landlord and dwelling registration.

Awaab's Law

Awaab's Law derives from Awaab Ishak, the two-year-old who tragically died from his prolonged exposure to mould at the socially rented home which he occupied with his parents. It led to a change in the law in which residential social landlords are now obliged by the Social Housing (Regulation) Act 2023 and Section 10A of the amended Landlord and Tenant Act 1985 and its associated regulations, to promptly address category hazards including damp and mould.

Sections 60 of the 2025 Act now further amends Section 10A of the Landlord and Tenant Act 1985 to extend Awaab's Law to all private tenancies, not only to those tenancies which are socially rented. However, these provisions will not be brought into effect immediately for private landlords and we await further announcement from the Government as regards implementation, together with bespoke regulations setting out the detail. In the meantime, Awaab's Law requires social housing providers to respond to emergency category hazards within 24 hours and to issues of damp or mould, within ten working days of the issue being reported. Once damp or mould or another category hazard has been identified, landlords have a further five working days to rectify the problem or, if it cannot be rectified, to move the family to suitable alternative accommodation.

Note Section 9A of the Landlord and Tenant Act 1985, which already places private landlords under a legal obligation to ensure that premises are fit for human habitation both at the beginning of the tenancy and throughout the subsistence of the tenancy. That duty remains unchanged.

Redress schemes

Provisions contained in the Housing Act 1996 first introduced a housing ombudsman for registered social landlords. Those provisions were strengthened by the Social Housing Regulation Act 2023. Currently, there is no equivalent Ombudsman scheme for private landlords. But that will change when Chapter 2 of Part 2 of the 2025 Act is brought into force.

Section 64 of the 2025 Act will enable the Secretary of State to make regulations requiring a residential landlord to be a member of a landlord redress scheme which enables tenant complaints to be independently investigated and determined, That scheme will not only be made available to existing tenants but also to prospective tenants. Regulations may also require a landlord to join a redress scheme before a dwelling is marketed for letting.

Section 65 enables the Secretary of State to make regulations setting out the powers available to the Ombudsman, which may include providing an apology or explanation, payment of compensation or such other actions as may be specified. Provisions may also enable landlords to be expelled from a scheme and prohibited from rejoining. And there may be fees payable for landlord registration within the scheme.

Section 67 of the Act creates offences if, following the imposition of a final penalty by the Ombudsman, the offending conduct continues after 28 days or if the person engages conduct which contravenes a different breach of regulations within five years from the date the relevant penalty was imposed.

Section 68 of the 2025 Act enables the Secretary of State to make regulations providing for the decision of an ombudsman to be enforceable as a court order. Section 66 enables a local housing authority to impose a financial penalty if satisfied beyond reasonable doubt that a person has breached regulations made under Section 64 or committed an offence under Section 67.

A decent homes standard (DHS)

The year 2035 might seem a lifetime away but that is the expected deadline when private landlords may be required to upgrade their properties to meet a new decent homes standard.

The idea of a decent homes standard, as a social housing aspiration, was first mooted in 2004 and updated in June 2006 through the Department for Communities and Local Government publication, "A Decent Home: Definition and Guidance for Implementation". Within that informal guidance, a 'decent home' was considered to have the following characteristics:

a It meets the current minimum safety standard for homes.
b It is in a reasonable state of repair.
c It has reasonably modern facilities and services.
d It provides a reasonable degree of thermal comfort.

Although the decent homes standard currently only applies to social lettings, Section 100(5) of the 2025 Act adds a new Section 2A to the Housing Act 2004 (power to set standards for qualifying residential premises), which enables the Secretary of State to make regulations specifying requirements to be met by qualifying residential premises. These new regulatory requirements may include:

a the state and repair of the premises,
b things to be provided for the safety, security or comfort of occupiers and
c the means of keeping the premises at a suitable temperature.

A new Section 2B to the Housing Act 2004, defines 'qualifying residential premises' as being either an HMO in England or a dwelling which is let on an assured tenancy or an assured agricultural occupancy or regulated tenancy.

Note also Section 101 of the 2025 Act, which relates specifically to military accommodation and which requires the Secretary of State to prepare and publish each year a report on the extent to which service family accommodation in England meets relevant standards and the work currently being undertaken to maintain and improve the standard of service family accommodation.

On 28 January 2026, the MHCLG published Consultation Outcome, 'The New Decent Homes Standard: Policy Statement'. The policy statement restates what constitutes the new Decent Homes Standard (DHS), namely:

Criterion A – A home must be free of the most dangerous hazards. This means the Category 1 hazards as assessed under the Housing Health and Safety Rating System (HHSRS).
Criterion B – A home must be in a reasonable state of repair.
Criterion C – A home must provide core facilities and services. This means:

- a kitchen with adequate space and layout,
- an appropriately located bathroom and WC,
- adequate external noise insulation and
- adequate size and layout of common entrance areas for blocks of flats.

Criterion D – A home must provide thermal comfort. This means ensuring that homes meet Minimum Energy Efficiency Standards [MEES].
Criterion E – A home should be free of damp and mould.

The policy statement then sets out in detail how private rented homes will be expected to meet these standards by 2035. Perhaps more important now for private landlords is the Government's proposals regarding implementation of the new decent homes standard as regards private rented accommodation. The following paragraphs in the Policy Statement would seem particularly relevant:

> *57. To achieve a lasting change for tenants, landlords will need to develop long-term plans to improve existing homes alongside building new homes and giving tenants a fairer deal – this will need investment and commitment*

over the next decade. That is why we are setting an implementation date of 2035 which is comparable to the 10-year target for the first DHS introduced in 2001 which required all social housing to meet set standards of decency by 2010.

58. However we encourage landlords to consider the benefits and feasibility of bringing properties up to the new DHS. They should not delay all action until the end of the implementation period.

59 Action to keep homes safe is a priority. While landlords will have until 2035 to bring their homes in line with new decency requirements, landlords will have to continue to meet their existing legal obligations to keep homes in repair and fit for habitation.

We now move to the following paragraphs in the Policy Statement which deal with enforcement of the DHS in the private rented sector:

69. In the private rented sector, the DHS will be enforced by local authorities. Part I of the Housing Act 2004 already requires PRS properties to meet Criterion A of the DHS by being free of Category 1 hazards. The Renters' Rights Act 2025 places a legal duty on private landlords to ensure their properties meet standards requirements to be set out in regulations. The intention is for those regulations together with regulations imposing higher Minimum Energy Efficiency Standards to require PRS properties to meet the other criteria of the DHS set out in this document."

72. Local authorities will have flexibility to take enforcement action in respect of DHS failures against a superior landlord in relation to a PRS property when appropriate (for example, the freeholder of a building containing a leasehold flat if the failures relate to common parts of the building).

73. In the private rented sector, DHS requirements will be divided into two tiers to support local authorities to prioritise the issues that present the greatest risk to tenants. If there are DHS failures under Criterion A – the presence of the most dangerous hazards – they will have a duty to take enforcement action and the ability to issue on the spot fines of up to £7,000. For all other DHS requirements, local authorities will have the power to take enforcement action but will not be under a legal duty to do so. Wider regulations, such as electrical, fire and gas safety requirements, will continue to apply.

76. The aim in setting a universal minimum standard is to create a baseline of quality for all rented homes in England. Some rented homes, however, in both tenures will fail to meet the new DHS. This is unavoidable. It is therefore important to have a system in place that differentiates between cases where landlords won't comply with the standard (willful non-compliance or failures of delivery, systems or governance that require regulation or enforcement), and where landlords either can't or shouldn't comply with some aspects of the standard.

79. In the private rented sector, local authorities should take into account the specific circumstances where aspects of the DHS can't be met when considering enforcement action. They will use their discretion to identify the appropriate best course of action in these instances:

- *where tenants refuse access*
- *where there are physical or planning factors that prevent compliance.*

80. There will be cases of specific tenure types, such as supported or temporary accommodation, where it is not appropriate for landlords to meet certain elements of the DHS because this is not in the best interest of the residents. An example may be accommodation for residents with particular health needs, where the provision of a kitchen for their own use is not appropriate.

81. We will provide clear guidance on applying the DHS to leasehold homes, including the respective responsibilities of freeholders and leaseholders, and continue engaging with stakeholders on how the DHS will apply to leasehold homes in a manner which is proportionate, effective, and fair for owner occupiers and landlord leaseholders.

In terms of 'Next steps', Paragraph 85 states that the MHCLG will, in due course, publish detailed guidance on the new DHS (including MEES) and bring forward the legislation and regulation to bring the new DHS into force within the social and private rented sectors by 2035.

Index

For Product Safety Concerns and Information please contact our EU representative GPSR@taylorandfrancis.com
Taylor & Francis Verlag GmbH, Kaufingerstraße 24, 80331 München, Germany

www.ingramcontent.com/pod-product-compliance
Ingram Content Group UK Ltd.
Pitfield, Milton Keynes, MK11 3LW, UK
UKHW022158190926
475702UK00003B/88

* 9 7 8 1 0 4 1 1 4 8 9 5 1 *